Mental Wellbeing

ISSUES

Volume 201

Series Editor

Lisa Firth

Independence

Educational Publishers

Cambridge

First published by Independence

The Studio, High Green

Great Shelford

Cambridge CB22 5EG

England

© Independence 2011

British Library Cataloguing in Publication Data

Mental wellbeing. -- (Issues ; v. 201)

1. Mental illness. 2. Mentally ill.

I. Series II. Firth, Lisa.

362.2-dc22

ISBN-13: 978 1 86168 573 5

Printed in Great Britain

MWL Print Group Ltd

CONTENTS

Chapter 1 Mental Health Issues

Cost of mental ill health in England exceeds £100 billion, new figures show	1
Factors that contribute to mental health problems in children and young people	2
Mental health: key points	5
Six out of ten Britons 'find it difficult to cope mentally'	6
Study reveals sleep duration link to mental ill health	7
Young people with parents affected by mental ill health	8
Younger people with dementia	10
Depression linked to dementia	12
Bipolar disorder	14
Schizophrenia	16
Dual diagnosis	17
Psychosis	18
Post Traumatic Stress Disorder (PTSD)	20

Chapter 2 Mental Illness Stigma

Stigma and discrimination in mental health	22
The reality of life with a mental health problem	24
Myths and facts about mental ill health	26
Fear of stigma stops employees with mental health problems from speaking out	27
New intervention to reduce self-stigma among persons with serious mental illness	28
With rights in mind	29
A manifesto for ending mental health stigma	31

Chapter 3 Surviving Mental Ill Health

How to improve your mental wellbeing	32
Mental health: strengthening our response	35
Young people could fall through the mental health care 'gap'	36
Only one in six people with mental illness receives recommended treatment	37
The Mental Health Act	38
Key Facts	40
Glossary	41
Index	42
Acknowledgements	43
Assignments	44

OTHER TITLES IN THE ISSUES SERIES

For more on these titles, visit: www.independence.co.uk

Stress and Anxiety ISBN 978 1 86168 314 4

Customers and Consumerism ISBN 978 1 86168 386 1

A Genetically Modified Future? ISBN 978 1 86168 390 8

The Education Problem ISBN 978 1 86168 391 5

Vegetarian and Vegan Diets ISBN 978 1 86168 406 6

Media Issues ISBN 978 1 86168 408 0

The Cloning Debate ISBN 978 1 86168 410 3

Sustainability and Environment ISBN 978 1 86168 419 6

The Terrorism Problem ISBN 978 1 86168 420 2

Religious Beliefs ISBN 978 1 86168 421 9

A Classless Society? ISBN 978 1 86168 422 6

Migration and Population ISBN 978 1 86168 423 3

Climate Change ISBN 978 1 86168 424 0

Euthanasia and the Right to Die
ISBN 978 1 86168 439 4

Sexual Orientation and Society
ISBN 978 1 86168 440 0

The Gender Gap ISBN 978 1 86168 441 7

Domestic Abuse ISBN 978 1 86168 442 4

Travel and Tourism ISBN 978 1 86168 443 1

The Problem of Globalisation
ISBN 978 1 86168 444 8

The Internet Revolution ISBN 978 1 86168 451 6

An Ageing Population ISBN 978 1 86168 452 3

Poverty and Exclusion ISBN 978 1 86168 453 0

Waste Issues ISBN 978 1 86168 454 7

Staying Fit ISBN 978 1 86168 455 4

Drugs in the UK ISBN 978 1 86168 456 1

The AIDS Crisis ISBN 978 1 86168 468 4

Bullying Issues ISBN 978 1 86168 469 1

Marriage and Cohabitation ISBN 978 1 86168 470 7

Our Human Rights ISBN 978 1 86168 471 4

Privacy and Surveillance ISBN 978 1 86168 472 1

The Animal Rights Debate ISBN 978 1 86168 473 8

Body Image and Self-Esteem ISBN 978 1 86168 484 4

Abortion – Rights and Ethics ISBN 978 1 86168 485 1

Racial and Ethnic Discrimination ISBN 978 1 86168 486 8

Sexual Health ISBN 978 1 86168 487 5

Selling Sex ISBN 978 1 86168 488 2

Citizenship and Participation ISBN 978 1 86168 489 9

Health Issues for Young People ISBN 978 1 86168 500 1

Crime in the UK ISBN 978 1 86168 501 8

Reproductive Ethics ISBN 978 1 86168 502 5

Tackling Child Abuse ISBN 978 1 86168 503 2

Money and Finances ISBN 978 1 86168 504 9

The Housing Issue ISBN 978 1 86168 505 6

Teenage Conceptions ISBN 978 1 86168 523 0

Work and Employment ISBN 978 1 86168 524 7

Understanding Eating Disorders ISBN 978 1 86168 525 4

Student Matters ISBN 978 1 86168 526 1

Cannabis Use ISBN 978 1 86168 527 8

Health and the State ISBN 978 1 86168 528 5

Tobacco and Health ISBN 978 1 86168 539 1

The Homeless Population ISBN 978 1 86168 540 7

Coping with Depression ISBN 978 1 86168 541 4

The Changing Family ISBN 978 1 86168 542 1

Bereavement and Grief ISBN 978 1 86168 543 8

Endangered Species ISBN 978 1 86168 544 5

Responsible Drinking ISBN 978 1 86168 555 1

Alternative Medicine ISBN 978 1 86168 560 5

Censorship Issues ISBN 978 1 86168 558 2

Living with Disability ISBN 978 1 86168 557 5

Sport and Society ISBN 978 1 86168 559 9

Self-Harming and Suicide ISBN 978 1 86168 556 8

Sustainable Transport ISBN 978 1 86168 572 8

Mental Wellbeing ISBN 978 1 86168 573 5

Child Exploitation ISBN 978 1 86168 574 2

The Gambling Problem ISBN 978 1 86168 575 9

The Energy Crisis ISBN 978 1 86168 576 6

Nutrition and Diet ISBN 978 1 86168 577 3

A note on critical evaluation

Because the information reprinted here is from a number of different sources, readers should bear in mind the origin of the text and whether the source is likely to have a particular bias when presenting information (just as they would if undertaking their own research). It is hoped that, as you read about the many aspects of the issues explored in this book, you will critically evaluate the information presented. It is important that you decide whether you are being presented with facts or opinions. Does the writer give a biased or an unbiased report? If an opinion is being expressed, do you agree with the writer?

Mental Wellbeing offers a useful starting point for those who need convenient access to information about the many issues involved. However, it is only a starting point. Following each article is a URL to the relevant organisation's website, which you may wish to visit for further information.

Cost of mental ill health in England exceeds £100 billion, new figures show

The cost of mental ill health in England is now £105.2 billion a year, according to an update published today by the Centre for Mental Health.

The figure includes the costs of health and social care for people with mental health problems, lost output in the economy, for example from sickness absence and unemployment, and the human costs of reduced quality of life.

The new calculation is an update of the £77.4 billion cost of mental ill health calculated by the Centre in 2003. The figure takes into account inflation since 2003 and the rising cost of health and social care.

'[Mental ill health] costs businesses more than £1,000 for every person they employ and has an impact on spending in every government department'

Centre for Mental Health joint chief executive Professor Bob Grove said: 'Mental ill health carries a heavy cost, especially for those who experience mental health problems and their families. It costs businesses more than £1,000 for every person they employ and has an impact on spending in every government department.

'Mental ill health is a fact of life. Every day, one in six of us experiences mental ill health, while one in 100 has a severe mental illness. It is vital that government, public services, businesses and communities respond well to mental ill health and do their bit to prevent both distress and discrimination.

'Parenting support to young families can cut the costs of conduct problems dramatically. Identifying depression at work can prevent loss of livelihood. Intervening early with children and young people in distress can have lifelong benefits and offer immediate gains in schools. And supporting people with severe or enduring mental health problems to make their own lives better can radically reduce disability and dependence.

'The Government's forthcoming mental health strategy is an opportunity to put mental health at the heart of public policy and the Big Society. By tackling the stigma of mental ill health, by intervening early and by doing what works to help people to fulfil their potential, we can cut the £105 billion cost of mental ill health dramatically and improve quality of life for all.'

3 October 2010

⇨ The above information is reprinted with kind permission from the Centre for Mental Health. Visit www.centreformentalhealth.org.uk for more information.

CENTRE FOR MENTAL HEALTH

Factors that contribute to mental health problems in children and young people

Information from Mind.

Asylum seekers and refugees

Asylum seekers and refugees have most often left their country of origin because of war, instability or because their human rights have been abused. Children and young people who arrive in this country under such circumstances face an uncertain future. They face difficulties such as language barriers and racism from the host community. Children will have lost all that was familiar to them, including family, friends and culture. Their mental wellbeing may have been affected by witnessing atrocities, or they may have been victims themselves.

Further information can be obtained from the health for asylum seekers & refugee's portal (www.harpweb.org.uk) and the Refugee Council (www.refugeecouncil.org.uk).

Bereavement

Children may experience the death of a grandparent, parent or sibling. While some appear to cope well, others may face a more complicated or unresolved kind of grief, which may be long and lead to depression and other kinds of mental health problems. Mind's booklet *Understanding bereavement* discusses the issues relating to bereavement in children and gives details of organisations that provide information and direct support for children coping with bereavement. Winston's Wish is a charity specifically for bereaved children and young people (www.winstonswish.org.uk).

Black and minority ethnic groups

Young people who experience racism or discrimination on account of their race, colour or religion are at increased risk of developing mental health problems. Families may experience racism or prejudice in housing, education or employment, compounding disadvantage. Stereotyping can lead to racist comments or even violence. Young people from minority ethnic groups may feel isolated and lack a sense of belonging. Young people of mixed parentage may experience additional identity and peer-related issues. Black and minority ethnic young people are over-represented in the mental health system, and they may experience forms of institutional prejudice that affect their future life chances. South Asian young women are more likely to attempt suicide than young men and women from other minority ethnic groups.

Mind has produced factsheets about different minority ethnic groups living in Britain. The Mental Health Foundation also provides information, and the website (www.mentalhealth.org.uk) has links to relevant organisations. YoungMinds (www.youngminds.org.uk) provides information specifically relating to young people.

Bullying

For most young people, being bullied is a transient experience; however, severe or persistent bullying can have long-lasting and devastating effects on a young person's mental health. The emotional consequences of bullying include a sense of inferiority, helplessness and fear. Above all, bullying is an attack on a child's self-esteem. The young person may feel worthless and a failure. Sleep can be affected, often punctuated by bad dreams and nightmares. Persistent bullying can lead to self-harm and has been associated with suicidal ideation. The charity Kidscape (www.kidscape.org.uk) was established to tackle bullying and sexual abuse of children.

MIND

Disability

Children and young people who have a physical disability often face isolation from other children, and may experience low self-esteem. They may also become depressed or feel anxious about the future and their relationships. The Disability Discrimination Act recognises that mental health problems are not confined to those with physical or sensory impairment. Mind has produced a booklet, *Disabled people and mental health support services,* and a briefing paper, *Legal briefing: Disability Discrimination Act.*

Divorce and separation

A significant number of children and young people see their parents divorce or separate. In most cases, they are able to manage this transition well, especially when they are supported by adults and friends in their lives. However, when a child is less resilient or support is not available, they may begin to experience difficulties at school, and some become aggressive. A child may go through a process akin to mourning following their parents' divorce or separation. Parents may be unable to offer the kind of support the child needs, and the child's world and security may be severely affected, leaving him or her anxious, angry and insecure about the future. A child may also experience denial and strong emotions such as guilt, shame, abandonment and rejection. YoungMinds, the Royal College of Psychiatrists (www.rcpsych.ac.uk) and Relate (www.relate.org.uk) all produce useful leaflets and advice about the effects of divorce/separation on children, and how to help.

Domestic violence

Children who witness domestic violence may find themselves in a state of constant fear and anxiety for the safety of a parent, or indeed their own wellbeing. They may experience a sense of loss for 'normal' family life. They may feel angry towards one or both parents and may be confused about where their loyalties lie. They may express anger through aggression towards peers and adults, although girls are more likely to 'internalise' their feelings. Relationships are inevitably affected and children may become withdrawn and isolated or try to dominate others in an attempt to control their world, which mostly feels out of control.

The charity Women's Aid (www.womensaid.org.uk) is the key national charity working to end domestic violence against women and children.

Emotional, sexual or physical abuse and neglect

Children who have been physically abused live in constant fear of the abuse happening again.

Emotional abuse often takes the form of humiliation, belittling, rejecting, showing little interest in a child and constant criticism. It is sometimes associated with parents who misuse alcohol, street drugs or other substances. Long-term emotional abuse can have a more debilitating effect on a young person's development.

Sexual abuse is often accompanied by confusion, shame and feeling dirty. Young people who have been sexually abused sometimes self-harm and may even attempt suicide. Long-term effects on the mental health of young people who have been abused include relationship problems (especially the fear of intimacy), and self-hatred may continue well into adult life. Sexual abuse is also linked with promiscuous behaviour and prostitution. Sometimes a child may fear that they too will become an abuser.

Any adult who works with children or young people and who suspects that a young person may be at risk or has been abused must share this information with an appropriate agency, e.g. social services.

Mind has produced a resource factsheet on sexual abuse which provides details of organisations that provide support and information for people who have been abused.

Kidscape, ChildLine (www.childline.org.uk), the NSPCC (www.nspcc.org.uk) and YoungMinds all provide information and support.

Gay and lesbian young people

Adolescence can be particularly challenging for gay, lesbian, bisexual and transgender young people. This is the time when young people form personal identities, and a young person's mental health may suffer if they do not get adequate support from families and friends. Problems can be exacerbated by the prejudices of others and a society that is sometimes judgemental and condemning. As well as ridicule, young men and women may face real or imagined threats of violence as a result of homophobia. The young person is sometimes told that this is a 'phase' they will grow out of, which can result in denial or the suppression of feelings. Gay and lesbian young people are over-represented in statistics on self-harm, depression and suicide.

Two Mind publications which may also be useful are: *Understanding gender dysphoria* (web only) and *How to cope with doubts about your sexuality.* The Queer Youth Network (www.queeryouth.org.uk) and Stonewall (www.stonewall.org.uk) provide useful information and support.

Living in care

According to government figures from 2005 about 61,000 children were being looked after by local authorities, representing approximately 0.5 per cent of young people up to the age of 18 years. Some children and young people find themselves in care for short periods while others are placed long term; some children are adopted into new families.

Children find themselves in care for a variety of reasons: they may have experienced abuse or neglect, possibly because of alcohol or drug misuse by their parents. A parent may be unable to care for them for a variety of reasons, or may have died. Clearly, a child taken into care has to establish new relationships with peers and care workers or foster parents. Such children are more likely to come from disadvantaged homes where there has already been additional risk. By definition, children in care have often already experienced traumatic events in their lives, so it is not surprising that they are more likely to develop mental health problems than those in stable family environments. Sometimes the experience of care can contribute to a child's already fragile self. Continuity in the care of children is vital in the maintenance of good mental health.

Living with a parent with a mental health problem

Some children and young people live with a parent who has a serious mental illness, such as depression, personality disorder or schizophrenia. The child may be affected by their parent's often reduced capacity to cope as a parent, and also by the parent's illness directly. Both parents and children may feel isolated and unsupported, which can lead to distress. Furthermore, living with a parent with a significant mental illness increases the chances of a young person developing mental health problems themselves.

Mind has produced a booklet, *How to parent when you're in a crisis*. The Mental Health Foundation provides a wealth of information on parental mental illness.

Poverty

A close link between poverty and mental health problems is well established. This can work in two ways: people with low incomes are more likely to experience poor mental health, and those with mental health problems are more likely to be living in poverty. Low income is likely to compromise housing and educational opportunities and leads to generally poor living conditions. Children and young people's relationships are likely to suffer because of the stress associated with low income.

The Child Poverty Action Group and the Joseph Rowntree Foundation are involved in tackling child poverty.

Prison

The Prison Reform Trust has argued that too many young people with mental health problems end up in prison. As many as nine out of ten young people in prison are thought to have at least one mental health problem, and sometimes a combination of problems. These include personality disorder, psychosis, neurotic disorder or substance misuse; schizophrenia and bipolar disorder are also found. Many young people who end up in prison have already experienced multiple disadvantages and often not completed full-time education. Some young people in prison have experienced a range of traumas, including sexual abuse. A significant number have self-harmed or attempted suicide. Suicide and attempted suicide in prison by young men remains a serious concern. The experience of prison, the loss of liberty, being away from family and friends and threats of violence will tend to exacerbate already complex problems.

Children and young people also suffer when a parent or close family member is sent to prison. When a parent is incarcerated, the effect of such parent-child separation may be similar to a sudden bereavement. As well as possible practical problems relating to care, loss of income and the loss of the adult as a role model, children may experience a wide range of feelings, which at times can become quite overwhelming. A child may believe that 'they' have been 'bad', that they are to blame for what has happened, and therefore may be traumatised by feelings of guilt. They may become embarrassed or feel the stigma associated with imprisonment and are therefore less likely to seek support. This can also be the case when embarrassment is felt by the wider family and the child is affected by a 'code of secrecy', leaving them confused and frustrated. In addition, children and young people with a parent in prison may feel anger towards the adult who has let them down or apparently 'abandoned' them. More information can obtained from the Prison Reform Trust (www.prisonreformtrust.org.uk) and Rethink (www.rethink.org).

Young carers

It is difficult to get an accurate picture of the number of young people who are in a caring role, partly because much of this work is hidden and unrecognised and partly because young people do not often seek help with this role. However, looking after an ill parent or sibling places considerable strain on a child or young person. As well as experiencing physical problems, caused by lifting for example, the young person may face emotional and social problems such as isolation, stress and stigma because home life is different from that of their peers.

The Princess Royal Trust for Carers has established YCNet, a web forum for young carers (www.youngcarers.net).

⇨ The above information is reprinted from the Mind factsheet *Children, young people and mental health* © Mind 2008. Visit www.mind.org.uk for more information on a wide range of mental health topics.

© Mind 2008

MIND

Mental health: key points

Information from The King's Fund.

⇨ Mental health problems are very common. Estimates from research studies suggest that one in four people in the UK experiences a diagnosable mental health problem at some point during their life. Depression and anxiety disorders are the most common forms of mental health problems, and evidence indicates that around a third of people with depression and half of people with anxiety disorders do not receive any support or treatment from health services.

⇨ Mental heath was one of the previous government's top three clinical priorities, alongside cancer and heart disease. Since 2001–02, real terms investment in adult mental health services has increased by 44 per cent. Over 700 new community mental health teams have been created, and numbers of consultant psychiatrists and mental health nurses have increased by 64 per cent and 21 per cent respectively since 1997.

⇨ Most people with mental health problems are supported solely by GPs and other professionals working in primary care. Around ten per cent of patients with mental health problems are referred on to specialist teams.

⇨ In spite of the high profile given to mental health by the previous government, some challenges have proven difficult to address. For example, waiting times for psychological therapies remain high. This is currently being tackled through the Improving Access to Psychological Therapies programme, launched in 2007.

⇨ Dementia currently accounts for 66 per cent of all mental health service costs, and is an issue of increasing concern. The King's Fund report *Paying the Price: The cost of mental health care in England to 2026* estimated that the number of people with dementia will increase by 62 per cent from 2007 to 2026. The Department of Health's National Dementia Strategy, launched in February 2009, aims to see diagnoses being made at an earlier stage of the illness, and to improve the quality of care provided.

⇨ For those people with severe mental illnesses such as schizophrenia, the last 25 years have witnessed a major transformation in the way services are delivered, with care shifting from large inpatient institutions to community-based teams. The NHS Plan in 2000 introduced a range of new service types designed to meet the needs of people with mental health problems living in the community.

⇨ After several years of debate, the 2007 Mental Health Act introduced a number of reforms to the laws governing when and how a person can be detained for assessment and treatment of mental health problems. The most controversial element of this is the introduction of Community Treatment Orders, under which patients can be compelled to continue taking medication after discharge from hospital.

⇨ The previous government launched a new mental health strategy in 2009, known as 'New Horizons'. This marked a shift in direction, with greater emphasis being placed on promoting positive mental health and wellbeing across the whole population and preventing mental health problems from developing. The current government has not yet released details on its mental health strategy, but the focus on prevention and promotion is expected to remain.

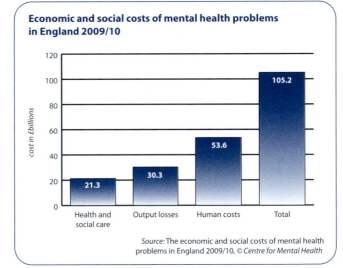

Economic and social costs of mental health problems in England 2009/10

Source: The economic and social costs of mental health problems in England 2009/10, © *Centre for Mental Health*

⇨ The costs to the NHS of mental ill health are forecast to rise over the coming years. The King's Fund report *Paying the Price: The cost of mental health care in England to 2026* estimated that expenditure will reach £47 billion a year by 2026, compared with £22.5 billion in 2007. This is due largely to a predicted rise in the number of people with dementia.

⇨ A key challenge for mental health services over the coming years will be to deliver better value for money without sacrificing quality of care. The King's Fund's 'Mental Health in a Cold Climate' project is exploring this issue, and will report later in 2010.

17 August 2010

⇨ The above information is reprinted with kind permission from The King's Fund. Visit www.kingsfund.org.uk for more information.

© *The King's Fund 2010*

THE KING'S FUND

Six out of ten of Britons 'find it difficult to cope mentally'

Information from Together.

Six out of ten of people (62%) in Great Britain (71% of women and 52% of men) have had at least one time in their life when they have found it difficult to cope mentally, according to the results of an online YouGov poll released today by the mental health charity Together.

Cracking up

The research, which was commissioned by Together to launch its annual Mental Wellbeing Week (8th–14th March), an annual event which promotes better mental health for all, found that stress (70%), anxiety (59%) and depression (55%) were the three most common difficulties encountered by the public.

But an astonishing 32% stated that they have actually been worried that they were 'cracking up' at one point or another (37% of women, 26% of men).

Affects everyone

Liz Felton, ex-Psychiatric Nurse and Together CEO says: 'This research shows that mental health and wellbeing is an issue relevant to most people, not just those with diagnosed issues. We hope the results go some way to try and reduce the "them and us" mentality about the topic that can lead to stigma, and perhaps prevents some people from seeking help, or talking about what they're going through when they need it.'

As part of Mental Wellbeing Week, people supported by the charity who have had difficulties themselves are reaching out to others by sharing the ten top pieces of advice they'd give to others having gone though it themselves on the charity's website, and acting as 'Voices of Experience' spokespeople.

Isolation

The Together research also revealed that of the respondents who did admit to experiencing difficulties, 69% had taken one step that saw them try and isolate themselves from the outside world or mask how they were feeling, rather than facing up to what was happening.

30% of respondents in this category (37% women, 22% men) had cancelled plans to see friends or made less of an effort to see them at difficult times, and an astonishing 18% of women stated that in at least one point in their lives, they'd wanted to go out but felt too nervous to do so. Whereas men (23%) were more likely than women (19%) to drink more alcohol than normal when feeling low.

According to Matthew Hyndman and Jo Smith-Kearney, Together 'Voices of Experience' spokespeople for the week, isolating yourself from the outside world is one of the worst things that you can do if you're having difficulty coping.

Jo Smith-Kearney, 'Voices of Experience' spokesperson for Together, says: 'My advice to others is that when you are feeling low you have to force yourself to make an effort and be as disciplined as you can, "duvet days" can be habit forming! You can lay in bed and rot, but you'll regret it afterwards.'

32% stated that they have actually been worried that they were 'cracking up' at one point

Matthew Hyndman, 'Voices of Experience' spokesperson for Together, says: 'I was bullied at university and it put me into a downward spiral to the point where most of my days were spent in the house staring at the television. I now realise this is the worst thing you can do, because the more isolated you become, the harder and more unimaginable it seems that you will ever have the courage to enter "normal" life again. It was like a vicious circle, but one I broke in the end.'

Commenting on the mental health charity Together's survey findings, Care Services Minister Phil Hope said:

'Other debilitating conditions like cancer or heart disease prompt sympathy and understanding. But mental health is all too often treated as taboo.

'As this survey makes clear, many of us will be affected by mental health problems at some point and that is why we are bringing forward a radical new approach which includes the national roll out of our successful talking therapies programme, NICE guidelines, new action on suicide prevention and a plan to tackle the stigma shrouding mental illness. The recently launched NHS Stressline also offers practical and emotional support for people suffering from anxiety, depression and stress.'
8 March 2010

⇨ The above information is reprinted with kind permission from Together. Visit www.together.org.uk for more.

© Together

Study reveals sleep duration link to mental ill health

Information from the George Institute for Global Health.

Healthy young adults who are sleeping less than five hours a night are three times more likely to develop mental ill health than those sleeping eight to nine hours, according to a new study undertaken by the George Institute for Global Health.

A survey of just under 20,000 17- to 24-year-olds across New South Wales, which ran for 18 months, revealed startling new evidence linking short sleep duration to mental ill health.

Mental ill health is more likely to develop into a chronic problem if a person is sleeping fewer hours than average

Professor Nick Glozier, lead author of the study, said 'The study has revealed a number of links between mental health problems and lack of sleep among young adults.' The study, published in the journal *Sleep*, also showed that mental ill health is more likely to develop into a chronic problem if a person is sleeping fewer hours than average.

According to Professor Glozier, 'Sleep disturbance is a key symptom in mental disorders such as depression and commonly an early sign or "prodrome" of the illness. There is also fairly consistent evidence that insufficient sleep also increases risk of cardiovascular illness, and can lead to weight gain in young people.'

'Sleep disturbance is a key symptom in mental disorders such as depression'

Professor Glozier added, 'Changes in lifestyle patterns are a contributing factor to these problems but it's evident that disrupted sleep patterns are a major contributor to many types of mental health conditions.'

The study was conducted as part of collaborative work undertaken by the University of Sydney's Brain and Mind Institute and the George Institute for Global Health.

Note

The fully published study can be found on http://www.journalsleep.org/AcceptedPapers/SP-047-10.pdf

⇨ The above information is reprinted with kind permission from the George Institute for Global Health. Visit www.georgeinstitute.org and www.journalsleep.org for more information on this and other related topics.

© George Institute for Global Health

THE GEORGE INSTITUTE FOR GLOBAL HEALTH

Young people with parents affected by mental ill health

'My mum has a mental illness, but no one told me why she was acting so weird. None of the doctors told me. It was scary. I had to find out for myself. They didn't think about how I was feeling and worrying.'

Synopsis

Mental ill health is often misunderstood; there is still great stigma associated with it. Research, guidance and practice highlights that children and young people who live and care for a parent or family member with mental ill health are often more reluctant to tell anyone about their family than those caring for someone with a physical disability.

Of the UK's 175,000 young carers, over 50,000 – 29% – are estimated to care for a family member with mental health problems

Like all young carers, children affected by mental ill health in the family experience many common impacts associated with a caring role, but they may experience further specific impacts, such as emotional impacts and safety issues.

The main focus of this article is on parental mental ill health, although a young carer may also be looking after a sibling. It is also important to remember that not all children whose family members have mental ill health will experience difficulties or be young carers.

The statistics

Of the UK's 175,000 young carers, over 50,000 – 29% – are estimated to care for a family member with mental health problems.

Between 25% and 50% of children living with a parent with severe mental ill health will experience some form of psychological disorder during their childhood or adolescence, and between 10% and 14% will be diagnosed with a psychotic illness during their lifetime.

Stigma

Young carers looking after a parent with mental ill health are often hidden because:

⇨ there is no visible illness or disability;

⇨ the illness may be episodic;

⇨ the young carer and/or the family is reluctant to seek support.

Some young carers go to great lengths to conceal the mental ill health within their families and make up excuses for their parent's behaviour. They can also experience significant confusion and emotional upheaval due to the episodic nature of mental ill health.

Parents may worry about discrimination and the effect their illness has on their child. Issues surrounding their child's schooling, such as behaviour or attendance problems, can add to stress which may further aggravate their illness. Parenting ability may also be impacted.

Young carers whose parents have severe mental ill health can live under large psychological stress which, in turn, can affect their own emotional health and wellbeing. Unemployment, poverty, familial stress and lack of support because the family fears intervention can all affect the young carer negatively. The young carer can be further impacted if the parent has to spend time in hospital and the family is separated.

Providing young carers with information

A parent's behaviour or even treatment is often not explained to the child or young person and this can lead to misunderstanding and confusion. Research indicates that age-appropriate information helps children to cope because:

⇨ children often imagine that things are worse than they are and so providing information therefore reduces fear;

⇨ understanding the illness can help the child empathise with and respect the person with the illness;

⇨ the child will realise it is not their fault.

The child's age, level of understanding, culture and the parent's wishes must be considered when providing information in all cases. Parents may also require help to understand why the child might need information about their mental ill health.

Additional caring responsibilities

Young carers of a parent with mental ill health can have further caring responsibilities, including significant emotional support such as keeping the parent company or cheering them up, and checking they take their medication.

The added emotional role is often the hardest for the child and can result in a role-reversal between parent and child.

Children with parents who have mental ill health can feel withdrawn, anxious, confused and worried, which can cause them to have behavioural difficulties and be violent or self-destructive. In some cases, children can adopt paranoid or suspicious behaviour as they believe their parents' delusions. These can all affect the child's education as they experience stigma and isolation, leading to them being victims of bullying, which in turn can lead to further isolation.

What do children say they need?

⇨ Good quality, age-appropriate information.

⇨ Someone whom they can trust to talk to and ask questions.

⇨ Someone to contact in a crisis.

⇨ Practical help.

⇨ To know their situation is not uncommon.

⇨ Issues to be discussed confidentially.

⇨ Support and understanding at school.

Safeguarding children affected by parental mental ill health

It is not inevitable that children are at risk of significant harm because they care for a parent with mental ill health. If you are concerned about the wellbeing of a child, school child protection procedures should be followed.

What can your school do?

⇨ The development of a whole-family approach is key to supporting young carers with parents affected by mental ill health. Your school should work with other agencies to enable this.

⇨ Consider offering the pupil, or referring the pupil for, an assessment following the Common Assessment Framework (CAF).

⇨ If there is another parent in the family who is not affected by mental ill health, involve them in support and consider also involving the child's extended family.

Dual diagnosis

Some parents can have both mental health ill-health and substance misuse issues. It is, therefore, important to maintain effective links between all agencies involved to provide extra support should they need it. In families affected either by mental ill health or substance misuse, it is important to listen to the child and monitor how this impacts on their wellbeing and development.

Some young carers go to great lengths to conceal the mental ill health within their families and make up excuses for their parent's behaviour

⇨ The above information is reprinted with kind permission from The Princess Royal Trust for Carers. The information is taken from *Pupils with parents affected by mental ill health,* part of a schools pack which was produced by The Princess Royal Trust for Carers in partnership with The Children's Society – from http://static.carers.org/files/20-mental-5089.pdf

© *The Princess Royal Trust for Carers*

Younger people with dementia

Information from Alzheimer's Society.

There are more than 16,000 younger people with dementia in the UK. However, this number is likely to be an underestimate, and the true figure may be up to three times higher. Data on the numbers of people with early onset dementia are based on referrals to services, but not all those with early onset dementia seek help in an early stage of the disease. The symptoms of dementia may be similar whatever a person's age, but younger people may have different needs, and their problems often require a different approach.

Types of dementia in younger people

'Younger people with dementia' is a term that includes anyone diagnosed with dementia under the age of 65. People also use the terms 'early onset dementia', 'young onset dementia' or 'working-age dementia'.

Only around one-third of younger people with dementia have Alzheimer's disease. Other common forms of dementia in younger people are:

⇨ Vascular dementia – Occurs when the blood vessels in the brain are deprived of oxygen. This can cause various symptoms, depending on the type of vascular damage.

⇨ Fronto-temporal lobar degeneration (FTLD) – Includes three clinical presentations: a behavioural form (fronto-temporal dementia) and two language forms (semantic dementia and progressive nonfluent aphasia). The same syndromes have also been known as Pick's disease. This term describes the pathology found in a subgroup of these patients.

⇨ Dementia with Lewy bodies – Caused by the build-up of tiny protein deposits in the brain. Symptoms tend to fluctuate, and people can develop the symptoms of Parkinson's disease and hallucinations.

⇨ Alcohol-related brain impairment – Often called Korsakoff's syndrome, this can occur in people who have regularly consumed a large amount of alcohol. It is caused by a lack of thiamine (vitamin B1) in the body, which affects the brain and other parts of the nervous system.

⇨ Rarer forms of dementia – Include prion disease (for example, Creutzfeldt-Jakob disease [CJD] – see Factsheet 427, *What is Creutzfeldt-Jakob disease [CJD]?*), or inherited conditions that can cause dementia (such as CADASIL syndrome). Around one-fifth of younger people with dementia have a rarer form of the condition.

People with other conditions, such as Parkinson's disease, multiple sclerosis, Huntington's disease or HIV and AIDS, may also develop dementia as part of their illness. People with Down's syndrome and other learning disabilities can also develop dementia at an early age.

Age as a barrier to care

Most people think of dementia as a condition affecting older people only. However, dementia can affect anyone, at any age. There is little awareness or understanding of people who develop dementia at an early age, and this can make it very difficult for younger people to access adequate support.

There are sometimes significant age-related barriers for younger people trying to get access to dementia services. Many dementia care services have a minimum age requirement of 65, and are not available to younger people. Where services are open to younger users, these may not be appropriate to their needs. Younger people often feel that they are made to 'fit in' to a service, rather than the service fitting their needs.

If no specialist services exist, younger people with dementia can find themselves lost between services, none of which will accept responsibility for their care.

Diagnosis

Getting an accurate diagnosis of dementia can take a very long time for younger people, often due to lack of awareness of dementia in people under 65. Medical professionals often misdiagnose younger people as being depressed, or as suffering from the effects of stress.

If a GP decides that specialist assessment is required, there can be confusion over the most appropriate consultant to refer to. Specialists in old age psychiatry are usually responsible for older people with dementia. Specialist diagnostic services, or named consultants for younger people with dementia, tend to be run by neurologists with a special interest in cognitive problems and dementia – however, due to lack of resources these are few and far between. Someone may be seen by a neurologist, a psychiatrist or an old-age psychiatrist.

This means that the route to diagnosis can be circuitous, and that younger people with dementia can receive very different levels of support from different doctors and professionals.

Specialist services

It is important that younger people with dementia have access to a range of specialist services, even at the

time of diagnosis. A small number of areas of the UK have named consultants with responsibility for younger people with dementia. A specialist diagnostic service should help people get access to care more quickly and easily. Alzheimer's Society is campaigning for similar services across the whole of the UK.

There are more than 16,000 younger people with dementia in the UK

Younger people also need specialist services following diagnosis. Even if dementia services accept younger users, the type of care they provide may not be appropriate. The needs of younger people with dementia and their friends and family are not just related to age. In many cases, people's fitness, activity and relationships matter as much as their age and diagnosis. In general, younger people with dementia are more likely to:

⇨ be in work at the time of diagnosis;

⇨ have dependent children or family;

⇨ be more physically fit and active;

⇨ have heavy financial commitments, such as a mortgage;

⇨ have a rarer form of dementia.

Younger people may have different concerns and interests to older people. A service set up for people of a different generation, where activities are planned for older people who are less physically active, is unlikely to meet the needs of younger people. Younger people with dementia require specialist services able to meet their complex needs.

The number of specialist services is growing, as more people come to understand the needs of younger people with dementia. In 1996 there were about 20 services in the UK that offered specialist support, and in 2004 there were over 120. While this figure is encouraging, progress is slow. Provision of services for younger people is variable around the country, and some regions still have few, if any, services.

Support from Alzheimer's Society

Because dementia in younger people is comparatively rare, it can be difficult to find other people who understand the situation. The Society can put younger people with dementia, their families or carers in contact with others in their local area, or in similar circumstances.

Many of our local services provide specialist support for younger people with dementia. If they do not, they can usually advise younger people on local services, and direct them to any specialist services that are available.

The Alzheimer's Society website has a dedicated section on younger people with dementia, at www.alzheimers.org.uk/ypwd. It also hosts an online discussion group called Talking Point, which has a dedicated group for younger people. To join the discussion, go to http://forum.alzheimers.org.uk

The Society can also provide support and information for younger people with dementia and their carers in a number of areas, including:

⇨ Work – Some people with dementia may want to continue working for some time after diagnosis, or they may wish to take early retirement if this is appropriate. Carers may also want to continue working, or may be concerned about giving up work to care full time. We can advise on some aspects of work and finances, but people with dementia and carers might need specialist advice. This should be available from a disability employment adviser at the local Jobcentre Plus, or from the local Citizens Advice Bureau.

⇨ Benefits – Younger people with dementia, and younger carers, need to make sure that they are receiving the benefits to which they are entitled. Contact the Benefit Enquiry Line on 0800 882 200.

⇨ Driving – Some people with dementia are able to drive safely for some time after their diagnosis, but there will be a point when they will have to stop driving. For many people with dementia, the decision to stop driving can be difficult.

⇨ Children – Younger people with dementia often have dependent children when they are diagnosed. It is important that children understand the condition, how it affects their parent and what changes to expect. Every child is different and will react in their own way.

Support for people with non-Alzheimer's dementias

Dementia can occur as a symptom of a number of conditions, including Down's syndrome or multiple sclerosis. Many of the relevant voluntary organisations provide good information on dementia, as it affects people with these conditions. In addition, Alzheimer's Society supports all people with dementia, whatever their age or diagnosis.

April 2010

⇨ The above information is reprinted with kind permission from Alzheimer's Society. Visit www.alzheimers.org.uk for more information on this and other related topics.

© *Alzheimer's Society*

Depression linked to dementia

Information from NHS Choices.

'Having depression may nearly double the risk of developing dementia later in life,' reported BBC News. It said that a 17-year study of nearly 1,000 elderly people found that 22% of those who were depressed at the start went on to develop dementia, compared with 17% of those who were not depressed.

This is a well-designed study and was accurately reported by the BBC. It has several strengths and adds to the evidence of a link between the two conditions.

However, as the researchers say, this does not necessarily mean that depression causes dementia and the reason for the association between the two conditions is still unclear. It is unknown if depression is a risk factor for dementia, whether it is an early sign of cognitive decline or if certain changes in the brain are associated with both conditions. Also, certain lifestyle factors were not measured by this study, such as poor diet, lack of physical activity and social interaction, and these may increase the risk of both depression and dementia.

Importantly, this study was in elderly people (average 79 years) and it is unknown if depression earlier in life would be associated with dementia in the same way. Further research is needed.

Where did the story come from?

The study was carried out by researchers from the University of Massachusetts in Worcester and Boston University, both in the US. It was funded by the US National Heart, Lung and Blood Institute, the National Institute on Aging and the National Institute of Neurological Disorders and Stroke. The study was published in the (peer-reviewed) medical journal *Neurology*.

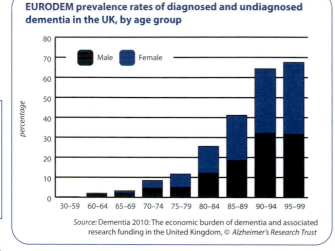

EURODEM prevalence rates of diagnosed and undiagnosed dementia in the UK, by age group

Source: Dementia 2010: The economic burden of dementia and associated research funding in the United Kingdom, © Alzheimer's Research Trust

The study was accurately reported on by the BBC, which was careful to explain that depression had not been proved to be a cause of dementia and that more research was needed to find out why the two conditions are linked. However, although the BBC mentions that the study was in elderly people, its story could be taken to imply that depression at any age is associated with dementia later. This study did not look at whether depression earlier in life is associated with later dementia.

The BBC also reported on another paper, published in the same journal, which found that the more times someone experienced depression, the higher their risk of dementia. This paper is not examined in this appraisal.

What kind of research was this?

This was a prospective cohort study, which aimed to examine a possible association between depression and dementia. The participants were recruited from the Framingham Heart study, a long-running cohort study that began in 1948 and was initially set up to investigate risk factors for cardiovascular disease.

Cohort studies are useful for looking at potential risk factors for conditions because they are able to follow large groups of people for many years and to assess how certain events (in this case, depression) might impact their health later. As a prospective study, its results are more reliable than a retrospective study. This is because it tracks people forward in time and can establish any relevant information at the start of the study, as opposed to relying on previous medical records or personal recall. There is also added strength in that it ensured that participants were free from cognitive impairment at the time their depression was assessed.

The researchers point out that some but not all previous studies have indicated a link between depression and cognitive impairment or dementia. Their research aimed to examine this possible association further over a longer follow-up period than previously achieved.

What did the research involve?

This particular study began in 1990, when 1,166 members of the original Framingham cohort attended for assessment. A total of 949 attendees were identified to be free of dementia and were included in the study. Of these, about 64% were women and the average age was 79 years.

The participants were assessed for depressive symptoms, using a validated depression scale that has a score ranging from 0−60, with higher scores reflecting greater depressive symptoms. Based on established guidelines, a score of 16 or over was used to define depression.

The researchers also recorded who was taking drug treatment for depression. Of the 949 participants, 125 (13.2%) were classified as depressed and a further 39 (4.1%) were taking anti-depressant medication.

The researchers followed up this group for up to 17 years (average follow-up was eight years). Those participants that developed dementia were identified using regular examinations every two years. For this, a well-established questionnaire was used to screen for cognitive impairment, together with other relevant findings from the primary care physicians, medical records, observations from clinic staff and personal observations from the participant and their family. Those with possible dementia had further neurological tests and were reviewed by a panel of specialists. Diagnoses of dementia were made using a validated diagnostic tool, and further assessments for Alzheimer's disease made using established criteria.

The researchers used validated statistical methods to analyse any potential link between depression at the beginning of the study and the subsequent development of dementia. Their analyses also took into account many things that can affect the risk of dementia, including age, sex, education, smoking habits, history of cardiovascular disease, diabetes and other relevant conditions.

What were the basic results?

During the 17-year follow-up, 164 participants developed dementia and 136 of these had Alzheimer's. A total of 21.6% of participants assessed as depressed at the start of the study went on to develop dementia, compared with 16.6% of those who were not depressed.

Overall, a total 21.6% of depressed participants developed dementia compared to 16.6% of non-depressed participants. This was equivalent to a 72% increased risk of dementia if the person had depression (Hazard ratio [HR] 1.72, 95%, Confidence interval [CI] 1.04–2.84).

For each ten-point increase in depressive symptoms there was a 46% increase in the risk of dementia (HR 1.46, 95% CI 1.18–1.79) and a 39% increase in risk of Alzheimer's disease (HR 1.39, 95%, CI 1.11–1.75).

When the figures were further adjusted to take account of vascular risk factors such as stroke and diabetes, depressed participants were found to have double the risk of dementia (HR 2.01, 95%, CI 1.20–3.31).

How did the researchers interpret the results?

The researchers say that their findings support previous studies that have suggested depression is a risk factor for dementia and Alzheimer's.

Conclusion

This is a well-designed study that has been reported on accurately by the BBC. It has numerous strengths, including a large sample size, long duration of follow-up, and validated methods of diagnosing dementia at follow-up.

There are several points to take into consideration.

As the authors themselves say, it is difficult to establish causality. Although the participants were assessed and found to be free from dementia at the beginning of the study, it is possible that in some of the people classified as having depression, their depressive symptoms were actually an early sign of dementia. It is also possible that both depression and dementia cause similar pathological changes in the brain (e.g. inflammation), or that an unmeasured biological factor may predispose a person both to dementia and to depression.

When assessing the relationship between dementia risk and depression, the researchers adjusted for numerous possible confounders, and this increases the reliability of the results. However, there is a possibility that an unmeasured confounder could be having an effect on the risk of both dementia and depression. The authors themselves acknowledge that they did not take into account lifestyle factors such as exercise, diet and social interaction.

The study did not include diverse ethnic groups and did not have psychiatric documentation of depression. The researchers were also unable to look at how long depression lasted and response to or adherence to antidepressant medication or other treatments.

It should also be pointed out that study participants had an average age of 79 at the start of the study when their depression status was assessed. It is possible that the same relationship between depression and dementia would not be observed if a cohort of young or middle-aged people with depression were followed into old age.

Nevertheless, this study adds more evidence that there is an association between depression in elderly people and risk of dementia. However, the reasons for the observed link are not completely clear, and further research would be needed to better establish whether this was a cause-and-effect relationship, or whether there was a similar disease process or causative factor underlying both conditions.

7 July 2010

⇨ Reproduced by kind permission of the Department of Health.

Bipolar disorder

Information from the National Institute of Mental Health.

What is bipolar disorder?

Bipolar disorder, also known as manic-depressive illness, is a brain disorder that causes unusual shifts in mood, energy, activity levels, and the ability to carry out day-to-day tasks. Symptoms of bipolar disorder are severe. They are different from the normal ups and downs that everyone goes through from time to time. Bipolar disorder symptoms can result in damaged relationships, poor job or school performance, and even suicide. But bipolar disorder can be treated, and people with this illness can lead full and productive lives.

Bipolar disorder often develops in a person's late teens or early adult years. At least half of all cases start before age 25. Some people have their first symptoms during childhood, while others may develop symptoms late in life.

Bipolar disorder is not easy to spot when it starts. The symptoms may seem like separate problems, not recognised as parts of a larger problem. Some people suffer for years before they are properly diagnosed and treated. Like diabetes or heart disease, bipolar disorder is a long-term illness that must be carefully managed throughout a person's life.

What are the symptoms of bipolar disorder?

People with bipolar disorder experience unusually intense emotional states that occur in distinct periods called 'mood episodes'. An overly joyful or overexcited state is called a manic episode, and an extremely sad or hopeless state is called a depressive episode. Sometimes, a mood episode includes symptoms of both mania and depression. This is called a mixed state. People with bipolar disorder may also be explosive and irritable during a mood episode.

Extreme changes in energy, activity, sleep and behaviour go along with these changes in mood. It is possible for someone with bipolar disorder to experience a long-lasting period of unstable moods rather than discrete episodes of depression or mania.

A person may be having an episode of bipolar disorder if he or she has a number of manic or depressive symptoms for most of the day, nearly every day, for at least one or two weeks. Sometimes symptoms are so severe that the person cannot function normally at work, school, or home.

Symptoms of bipolar disorder are described below.

Symptoms of mania or a manic episode include:

Mood changes

⇨ A long period of feeling 'high,' or an overly happy or outgoing mood.

⇨ Extremely irritable mood, agitation, feeling 'jumpy' or 'wired'.

Behavioural changes

⇨ Talking very fast, jumping from one idea to another, having racing thoughts.

⇨ Being easily distracted.

⇨ Increasing goal-directed activities, such as taking on new projects.

⇨ Being restless.

⇨ Sleeping little.

⇨ Having an unrealistic belief in one's abilities.

⇨ Behaving impulsively; taking part in a lot of pleasurable, high-risk behaviours, such as spending sprees, impulsive sex and impulsive business investments.

Symptoms of depression or a depressive episode include:

Mood changes

⇨ A long period of feeling worried or empty.

⇨ Lost interest in activities once enjoyed, including sex.

Behavioural changes

⇨ Feeling tired or 'slowed down'.

⇨ Having problems concentrating, remembering and making decisions.

⇨ Being restless or irritable.

⇨ Changing eating, sleeping or other habits.

⇨ Thinking of death or suicide, or attempting suicide.

How does bipolar disorder affect someone over time?

Bipolar disorder usually lasts a lifetime. Episodes of mania and depression typically come back over time. Between episodes, many people with bipolar disorder are free of symptoms, but some people may have lingering symptoms.

NATIONAL INSTITUTE FOR MENTAL HEALTH

Doctors usually diagnose mental disorders using guidelines from the *Diagnostic and Statistical Manual of Mental Disorders*, or DSM. According to the DSM, there are four basic types of bipolar disorder:

1 Bipolar I Disorder is mainly defined by manic or mixed episodes that last at least seven days, or by manic symptoms that are so severe that the person needs immediate hospital care. Usually, the person also has depressive episodes, typically lasting at least two weeks. The symptoms of mania or depression must be a major change from the person's normal behaviour.

2 Bipolar II Disorder is defined by a pattern of depressive episodes shifting back and forth with hypomanic episodes, but no full-blown manic or mixed episodes.

3 Bipolar Disorder Not Otherwise Specified (BP-NOS) is diagnosed when a person has symptoms of the illness that do not meet diagnostic criteria for either bipolar I or II. The symptoms may not last long enough, or the person may have too few symptoms, to be diagnosed with bipolar I or II. However, the symptoms are clearly out of the person's normal range of behaviour.

4 Cyclothymic Disorder, or Cyclothymia, is a mild form of bipolar disorder. People who have cyclothymia have episodes of hypomania that shift back and forth with mild depression for at least two years. However, the symptoms do not meet the diagnostic requirements for any other type of bipolar disorder.

Some people may be diagnosed with rapid-cycling bipolar disorder. This is when a person has four or more episodes of major depression, mania, hypomania or mixed symptoms within a year. Some people experience more than one episode in a week, or even within one day. Rapid cycling seems to be more common in people who have severe bipolar disorder and may be more common in people who have their first episode at a younger age. One study found that people with rapid cycling had their first episode about four years earlier, during mid to late teen years, than people without rapid cycling bipolar disorder. Rapid cycling affects more women than men.

Bipolar disorder tends to worsen if it is not treated. Over time, a person may suffer more frequent and more severe episodes than when the illness first appeared. Also, delays in getting the correct diagnosis and treatment make a person more likely to experience personal, social and work-related problems.

Proper diagnosis and treatment helps people with bipolar disorder lead healthy and productive lives. In most cases, treatment can help reduce the frequency and severity of episodes.

How is bipolar disorder diagnosed?

The first step in getting a proper diagnosis is to talk to a doctor, who may conduct a physical examination, an interview, and lab tests. Bipolar disorder cannot currently be identified through a blood test or a brain scan, but these tests can help rule out other contributing factors, such as a stroke or brain tumour. If the problems are not caused by other illnesses, the doctor may conduct a mental health evaluation. The doctor may also provide a referral to a trained mental health professional, such as a psychiatrist, who is experienced in diagnosing and treating bipolar disorder.

The doctor or mental health professional should conduct a complete diagnostic evaluation. He or she should discuss any family history of bipolar disorder or other mental illnesses and get a complete history of symptoms. The doctor or mental health professionals should also talk to the person's close relatives or spouse and note how they describe the person's symptoms and family medical history.

The first step in getting a proper diagnosis is to talk to a doctor

People with bipolar disorder are more likely to seek help when they are depressed than when experiencing mania or hypomania. Therefore, a careful medical history is needed to ensure that bipolar disorder is not mistakenly diagnosed as major depressive disorder, which is also called unipolar depression. Unlike people with bipolar disorder, people who have unipolar depression do not experience mania. Whenever possible, previous records and input from family and friends should also be included in the medical history.

How is bipolar disorder treated?

To date, there is no cure for bipolar disorder. But proper treatment helps most people with bipolar disorder gain better control of their mood swings and related symptoms. This is also true for people with the most severe forms of the illness.

Because bipolar disorder is a lifelong and recurrent illness, people with the disorder need long-term treatment to maintain control of bipolar symptoms. An effective maintenance treatment plan includes medication and psychotherapy for preventing relapse and reducing symptom severity.

⇨ The above information is reprinted with kind permission from the US-based National Institute for Mental Health. Visit www.nimh.nih.gov for more.

© National Institute for Mental Health

NATIONAL INSTITUTE OF MENTAL HEALTH

Schizophrenia

Information from mentalhealthcare.org.uk, a website for family members and friends of people with psychosis.

What is schizophrenia?

Schizophrenia is a serious mental illness. People who have schizophrenia often have what health professionals describe as 'positive symptoms' – delusions, hallucinations, disordered thinking – during episodes of psychosis. People with schizophrenia can also have what health professionals call 'negative symptoms'. They may have no energy and lose the motivation to do anything; they may lose interest in friends, family members and activities they previously enjoyed. They may also have memory problems and find it very hard to concentrate. They may no longer care about their personal appearance and become isolated and withdrawn. People with schizophrenia may not accept that they are unwell and may not want to ask for help or treatment.

The experiences and symptoms each person has will differ and last for different periods of time. Some people are unwell for only a short period. Others experience the symptoms for months, or even years. A few people have just one episode of psychosis in their lives. Many people have episodes of psychosis that come and go over time. A small number of people have distressing symptoms that continue.

The symptoms of psychosis diminish and often disappear following treatment with medication and talking therapies. However, antipsychotic drugs don't work for some people. Their illness is then called 'treatment-resistant', or 'refractory', schizophrenia.

Sometimes, antipsychotic medication controls the symptoms of psychosis, but people still experience the negative symptoms of schizophrenia, and these may last for some time.

People with schizophrenia often also have depression, anxiety or a personality disorder. Between five and ten per cent will take their own lives.

Who gets schizophrenia?

About one in every 100 people will have schizophrenia at some time in their lives. People can develop schizophrenia at any age, but the illness usually starts for men when they are in their late teens or early 20s. Women tend to develop schizophrenia when they are slightly older, in their late 20s. A small number of people develop schizophrenia in middle age. There is now some evidence to show that children in their teenage years or younger can also have symptoms.

Anyone can get schizophrenia, though children of a parent who has the illness are slightly more likely to become unwell. Even though genes play a part in the development of schizophrenia, there is no single cause and many contributing factors. Just because one person in the family has schizophrenia doesn't mean that other family members will inevitably develop the illness.

Early signs

Sometimes the illness starts suddenly with an acute, and often frightening, episode of psychosis.

However, a first episode of psychosis is often heralded by what health professionals call a 'prodromal period' when people's behaviour begins to change.

People are often depressed or anxious, may find it difficult to concentrate or have problems remembering things, stop seeing their friends, act in a strange and uncharacteristic way, become less interested in study, work or hobbies and care less about how they look. They may become socially withdrawn and spend much more time alone.

They also sometimes have experiences resembling the symptoms of psychosis – hearing voices every now and then, being occasionally suspicious and paranoid, for example. Research has shown that up to half the people who have these sort of experiences go on to have a first episode of psychosis.

After an initial episode, a large proportion of people get better with treatment. Others will improve but may have further episodes.

Research has shown that the more quickly treatment is given, the better people recover from the symptoms. People who don't access mental health services when they first get symptoms get better more slowly, or are less likely to get completely better, and have an increased risk of relapse in the future.

Living with schizophrenia

Schizophrenia can severely affect people's lives and the lives of their families. In addition to the distressing and often frightening symptoms, people with schizophrenia may find it difficult to get jobs, make friends and have relationships. Other people's fear and misunderstanding of the illness often leads to discriminatory practices that leave people with schizophrenia even more socially isolated.

Physical health problems

People with schizophrenia are more at risk of physical health problems, including weight gain, high blood pressure, heart disease and diabetes. These problems

are caused by changes in lifestyle as a result of the symptoms of the illness, and can also be a side effect of antipsychotic medication. People with schizophrenia are more likely to smoke and less likely to take exercise, for instance.

GPs should check the physical health of people with schizophrenia once a year, including their weight, blood pressure, blood sugar and cholesterol levels. People should be given treatment for any physical health problems and encouraged to raise any such problems with their GP.

People with schizophrenia are more likely to die younger than other people because of these increased rates of physical health problems.

8 February 2010

⇨ Information from mentalhealthcare.org.uk, a website for family members and friends of people with psychosis. www.mentalhealthcare.org.uk is created by the Institute of Psychiatry, King's College London, and South London and Maudsley NHS Foundation Trust.

© *mentalhealthcare.org.uk*

Dual diagnosis

One US study has found that 50% of people with mental health problems were also abusing drugs or alcohol at a problematic level. Very little research has been conducted in the UK: however, it is a very real problem here.

What does dual diagnosis mean?

It is a relatively new term originating from the States that describes people who are diagnosed as having problematic drug use or alcohol abuse and a serious mental illness (often schizophrenia). This can take two forms:

⇨ Those who have firstly been diagnosed with a serious mental health problem who are later also found to be using recreational drugs that may have an adverse effect on their illness; for example, a schizophrenic who takes speed. Their drug-induced psychosis may well mask real mental health problems. One UK study found that 40% of people with schizophrenia also abused drugs/alcohol.

⇨ Those who have been diagnosed with drug dependency which triggers/leads to a later diagnosis of a mental health problem. This is more likely with excessive use of stimulants (speed, coke and crack).

More recently the term 'complex needs' has begun to be used to describe the social needs of someone with dual diagnosis. It is an attempt to use a more holistic way of both diagnosing and treating the problem.

UK figures

A study conducted by Maudsley Hospital, London, interviewed people diagnosed with schizophrenia and found a lower number of dual diagnoses than in the States.

Another study, this time of people with mental health problems in the criminal justice system, found a dual diagnosis rate of more than 50%.

Some UK drug service experts estimate that up to a third of those who come into contact with drug services will also have a mental health problem of some kind.

Why is it a problem?

The combination of recreational drug use and symptoms of mental illness means that it's very difficult to tell whether there is a real problem, or just simply the side effects of recent drug use. The symptoms of schizophrenia or manic depression can be almost identical to those someone displays when they are intoxicated, suffering from amphetamine psychosis, or withdrawing from excessive dependant drug use.

It is also quite common for people with added stress or the beginnings of a mental illness to try to escape their problems and symptoms through alcohol or drugs, although often it only makes the initial problem worse.

A period of three to six weeks abstaining from drug use is generally needed to help make a clear diagnosis. However, this is often easier said than done, as some may not want to give up drugs, or may not be able to. If managed, and the symptoms vanish, it was merely a result of the drug use. However, if symptoms remain it means that either there is a real mental illness needing treatment, or the person has not stopped taking drugs.

Dual diagnosis is also a significant factor in suicide figures, as during the waiting time to decide whether the person's symptoms are drug-induced or an indication of a mental health problem, the person's illness may worsen and they could become more at risk of a suicide attempt. It is a fairly impossible situation for mental health professionals, and while they are trying to work out a better solution to dual diagnosis, the risks for young people are high.

⇨ The above information is reprinted with kind permission from TheSite.org. Visit www.thesite.org for more information.

© *TheSite.org*

Psychosis

Forget the ignorance, fear and tacky tabloid hype. What does psychosis really mean?

What is psychosis?

Psychosis is a psychiatric term used to describe experiences or beliefs you may have that are not shared with other people. These can take the form of hallucinations or delusions in which you might be unable to distinguish between your own intense thoughts and reality. Your thoughts might jump around and you may find it difficult expressing yourself in a way that others can understand. You may have little insight into the condition, and not recognise that you are ill. If you have psychotic experiences it may lead to a doctor diagnosing a mental illness such as schizophrenia or manic depression.

What are the symptoms?

You might have hallucinations: hearing, seeing or smelling things that others don't experience. The most common form of hallucination that people have is hearing voices in their head, but you could taste or

smell things that other people can't, or have physical sensations with no obvious cause. These experiences can be very distressing, particularly if the voices in your head are saying unpleasant things or encouraging you to do things you don't want to.

> ### If you have ongoing problems with psychosis, it is most likely that you are experiencing some form of mental health problem

You might experience delusions: having unusual beliefs that are not shared by other people, for example that you are rich, famous or powerful. You could believe that other people are controlling your mind: placing thoughts in your head or controlling your behaviour. You could feel paranoid, powerless and not in control of your own behaviour.

Who experiences it?

Anyone could have a brief, one-off psychotic experience as a result of alcohol or drug use, jet-lag or lack of sleep, or as a result of physical illness or fever. However, if you have ongoing problems with psychosis, it is most likely that you are experiencing some form of mental health problem. Psychosis is a common feature of mental illnesses such as schizophrenia, manic depression and schizoaffective disorder, but can also be a symptom of severe depression or post-natal depression.

What causes it?

There is no one cause of psychosis. For some people psychosis is triggered because the person has a diagnosable mental illness such as schizophrenia or manic depression. For others, it appears to be caused by a combination of factors, including: genetics; changes in brain chemistry; stressful life events, or usage of street drugs. Overall, it appears likely that some people may be born with a genetic predisposition towards psychosis but it takes stressful life events or experiences to trigger the onset of symptoms.

What can be done?

The first step towards recovery from any illness is usually to recognise that there is a problem and to seek help.

However, people experiencing psychosis often do not have the insight to recognise that they have a problem that can be treated. If this is the case, friends or family may have a role in encouraging the person to seek help. The first point of contact would usually be a GP who may be able to diagnose the underlying cause, prescribe drug treatment, or refer the person to a psychiatrist or psychologist for more intensive treatment.

Psychosis is usually treated with antipsychotic drugs, which have a tranquillising effect and aim to reduce distressing psychotic symptoms such as delusions and hallucinations

Psychosis is usually treated with antipsychotic drugs, which have a tranquillising effect and aim to reduce distressing psychotic symptoms such as delusions and hallucinations. Some people may experience unpleasant or distressing side effects from medication that makes them reluctant to take the drugs. If someone stops taking their medication it can lead to relapse. It is important to discuss with your doctor any problems or side effects you may be having from your prescribed drugs, as they may be able to help.

Other forms of treatment are known as talking treatments; these include counselling, cognitive behaviour therapy (CBT) and psychotherapy. If a person is very distressed, they may be admitted to hospital for treatment. People are usually encouraged to go to hospital as voluntary patients, but sometimes if someone's behaviour is very disturbed, usually during psychotic episodes, they can be admitted to hospital against their will under the Mental Health Act 1983.

Who can help?

Friends and family can help by encouraging the person to seek treatment and support. They can offer general support and show the person that they are cared for. It is important to ensure that you don't say anything that might collude with delusional beliefs or feed any paranoia, as this can worsen the situation. It can be quite distressing being with someone having a psychotic experience, so friends and family might wish to seek some support for themselves too. Many organisations can provide advice, information and practical or emotional support for people experiencing psychosis, their friends and family. These include mental health and drug charities, helplines, counselling and therapy services, social services, GPs and the health service.

⇨ The above information is reprinted with kind permission from TheSite.org. Visit their website at www.thesite.org for more information on this and other related topics.

© TheSite.org

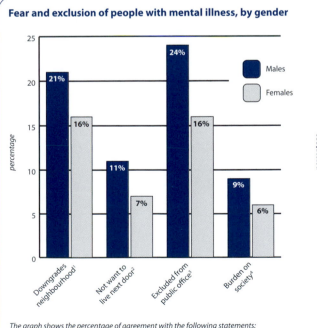

Fear and exclusion of people with mental illness, by gender

Males: Downgrades neighbourhood[1] 21%, Not want to live next door[2] 11%, Excluded from public office[3] 24%, Burden on society[4] 9%
Females: Downgrades neighbourhood[1] 16%, Not want to live next door[2] 7%, Excluded from public office[3] 16%, Burden on society[4] 6%

The graph shows the percentage of agreement with the following statements:
[1] *Locating mental health facilities in a residential area downgrades the neighbourhood.*
[2] *I would not want to live next door to someone who has been mentally ill.*
[3] *Anyone with a history of mental problems should be excluded from taking public office.*
[4] *People with mental illness are a burden on society.*

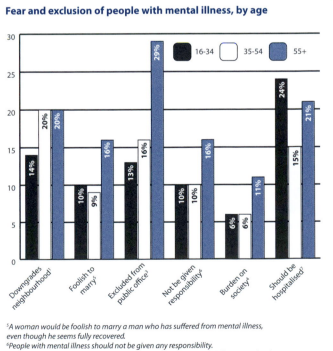

Fear and exclusion of people with mental illness, by age

16-34, 35-54, 55+

Downgrades neighbourhood[1]: 16-34 14%, 35-54 20%, 55+ 20%
Foolish to marry[5]: 16-34 10%, 35-54 9%, 55+ 16%
Excluded from public office[3]: 16-34 13%, 35-54 16%, 55+ 29%
Not be given responsibility[6]: 16-34 10%, 35-54 10%, 55+ 16%
Burden on society[4]: 16-34 6%, 35-54 6%, 55+ 11%
Should be hospitalised[7]: 16-34 24%, 35-54 15%, 55+ 21%

[5] *A woman would be foolish to marry a man who has suffered from mental illness, even though he seems fully recovered.*
[6] *People with mental illness should not be given any responsibility.*
[7] *As soon as a person shows signs of mental disturbance, they should be hospitalised.*

Source: Attitudes to mental illness 2010 research report, *March 2010,* © The Department of Health-funded anti-stigma programme, Crown Copyright

THESITE.ORG

Post Traumatic Stress Disorder (PTSD)

Information on service-related mental ill health.

Post Traumatic Stress Disorder (PTSD) is a complex and debilitating condition that can affect every aspect of a person's life.

It is a psychological response to the experience of an event (or events) of an intensely traumatic nature. These type of events often involve a risk to life – one's own or that of one's colleagues.

It is a condition that can affect anyone, regardless of age, gender or culture.

PTSD has been known to exist since ancient times, albeit under the guise of different names.

Although PTSD was first brought to public attention by war veterans, it can result from any number of traumatic incidents. The common denominator is exposure to a threatening event

During the First World War it was referred to as 'shell shock'; as 'war neurosis' during WWII, and as 'combat stress reaction' during the Vietnam War. In the 1980s the term Post Traumatic Stress Disorder was introduced – the term we still use today.

Although PTSD was first brought to public attention by war veterans, it can result from any number of traumatic incidents. The common denominator is exposure to a threatening event that has provoked intense fear, horror or a sense of helplessness in the individual concerned.

The sort of traumatic events that might be experienced by members of the general public include physical assault, rape, accidents or witnessing the death or injury of others – as well as natural disasters, such as earthquakes, hurricanes, tsunamis and fires.

In the case of serving personnel, traumatic events mostly relate to the direct experience of combat, to operating in a dangerous war-zone, or to taking part in difficult and distressing peace-keeping operations.

PTSD: common symptoms

PTSD is characterised by three main symptom clusters. These are re-experiencing, avoidance and hyper-arousal symptom clusters.

Re-experiencing symptoms

Individuals with PTSD repeatedly relive the event in at least one of the following ways:

⇨ Intrusive unwanted memories of the traumatic event.

⇨ Unpleasant nightmares which comprise replays of what happened.

⇨ Flashbacks where they may suddenly act or feel as if they are reliving the event.

⇨ They become emotionally upset if something reminds them of the traumatic experience.

⇨ Palpitations, sweating, feeling tense or shaky if they are reminded about their traumatic experience.

COMBAT STRESS

Avoidance symptoms

People with PTSD try to avoid thoughts and feelings related to the traumatic event. They find it extremely difficult at times, as the traumatic images and memories intrude spontaneously. Symptoms include:

⇨ Avoidance of activities, places or people which remind them of their trauma.

⇨ Difficulty remembering exactly what happened during exposure to their traumatic event (this reflects the intense fear at the time of exposure).

⇨ Becoming less interested in hobbies and activities that they used to enjoy before the traumatic event.

⇨ Feeling detached and estranged from people, and feeling that nobody understands them – a tendency to isolate themselves.

⇨ Becoming emotionally numb, and having trouble experiencing their feelings.

⇨ A sense of futility in relation to their future and feeling that somehow they will be struck down by yet another disaster or tragedy.

Hyper-arousal symptoms

Hyper-arousal symptoms cause problems with relationships, especially problems generated by irritability and anger. They include:

⇨ Great difficulty falling or staying asleep.

⇨ A tendency to become irritable and angry at the slightest provocation and for trivial reasons.

⇨ A tendency to become aggressive, verbally or physically, or to become violent towards themselves or others.

⇨ Great difficulty concentrating, and concentration usually requires effort.

The common denominator [in PTSD sufferers] is exposure to a threatening event that has provoked intense fear, horror or a sense of helplessness in the individual concerned

---

⇨ Remaining especially alert and watchful (hyper-vigilant).

⇨ Looking for signs of danger in their environment and in an exaggerated way; they are tuned in to any sign that they might perceive as threatening.

Commonly associated symptoms

The other symptoms that are commonly associated with PTSD relate to feelings of guilt, and difficulty relating to authority figures.

Guilt can take two forms:

⇨ Guilt in relation to what one should or should not have done during the traumatic exposure.

⇨ Survivor guilt: while the individual survived relatively intact (physically, at least), others involved in the traumatic experience did not.

In many traumatic exposures, the individual may perceive that the system or hierarchy has let them down, and therefore anger and hostility can be a major factor in the presentation of PTSD.

⇨ The above information is reprinted with kind permission from Combat Stress. Visit www.combatstress.org.uk for more information.

© Combat Stress

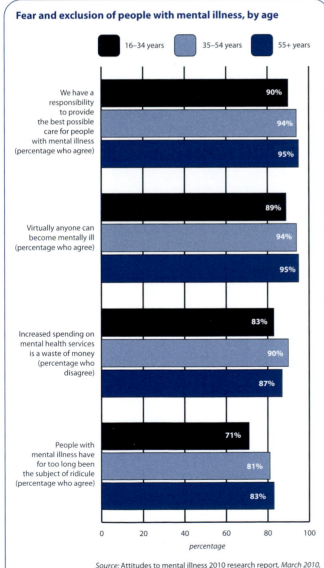

Fear and exclusion of people with mental illness, by age

- 16–34 years
- 35–54 years
- 55+ years

We have a responsibility to provide the best possible care for people with mental illness (percentage who agree)
- 90%
- 94%
- 95%

Virtually anyone can become mentally ill (percentage who agree)
- 89%
- 94%
- 95%

Increased spending on mental health services is a waste of money (percentage who disagree)
- 83%
- 90%
- 87%

People with mental illness have for too long been the subject of ridicule (percentage who agree)
- 71%
- 81%
- 83%

percentage (0, 20, 40, 60, 80, 100)

Source: Attitudes to mental illness 2010 research report, March 2010,
© The Department of Health-funded anti-stigma programme, Crown Copyright

COMBAT STRESS

Stigma and discrimination in mental health

Nearly nine out of ten people (87%) with mental health problems have been affected by stigma and discrimination.

More than two thirds of people with mental health problems (71%) say they have stopped doing things they wanted to do because of stigma. Even more (73%) say they have stopped doing things they wanted to do because of fear of stigma and discrimination. People with mental health problems say that stigma and discrimination affect all aspects of their lives: work, education, friendships, community participation, going to the shops, going out to the pub, talking to other people about their mental health problems. 53% of carers of people with mental health problems also say they feel unable to do things they want to do because of stigma and discrimination, and 43% say they are unable to do things because of fear of stigma and discrimination. Stigma and fear can stop people (and people from BME communities in particular) seeking help at an early stage for their mental health problems. Two-thirds of people with mental health problems live alone – four times more than the general population. More than 50% of people with mental health problems have poor social contact, as defined by the Oslo Social Support Scale, compared with 6% of the general population. People with mental health problems see fewer friends regularly – between one and three in an average week, compared with the four to six friends reported by the general population.

Crime and violence

People with mental health problems say that stigma and discrimination leave them vulnerable to violence. In one survey, 71% of respondents had been victimised in the community at least once in the past two years and believed this was related to their mental health history. Nearly nine out of ten respondents living in local authority housing had been victimised. Nearly half (41%) said they were subjected to repeated bullying. Yet 30% of victims of crime in the community told no one what had happened to them, and 45% of those who were victims of crime in hospital did not tell a member of staff – 36% of those who did not report the crime said they didn't think they would be believed.

Employment

People with severe mental health problems have a lower rate of employment than any other disabled group but they are more likely than any other group with disabilities to want to have a job. Up to 90% say they would like to work, compared with 52% of disabled people generally. Fewer than one in four (21%) people with a disabling mental health condition are in paid employment, compared with 47% of all disabled people. Employment rates for those with a more serious mental health condition are even lower and have fallen steadily over four decades. Fewer than four in ten employers say that they would consider employing someone with a history of mental health problems (compared with six out of ten who would consider employing someone with a physical disability). Nearly three in five (59%) employees in the UK say they would feel uncomfortable talking to their line manager about it if they had a mental health problem. Only 9% would feel very comfortable about discussing a mental health problem and 24% would feel fairly comfortable. The main reason is fear of losing their job (26%), followed by concern about their colleagues finding out about their diagnosis (19%). Nearly one in five (18%) employees say

NATIONAL MENTAL HEALTH DEVELOPMENT UNIT

they would be concerned that their line manager would think they were 'mad', and that they would be overlooked for promotion (16%). 92% of the UK public believe that disclosing a history of mental health problems would damage a person's career. Careers considered most vulnerable to damage include doctors (56%), emergency services personnel (54%) and teachers (48%). Only 21% feel that having a history of mental health problems could damage the career of an MP. More than half of the UK public (56%) would not offer an interviewee a job, even if they were the best candidate, if they disclosed that they had a history of depression – 17% because they thought the person would be unreliable, 10% because they thought they would be blamed if the person then took time off sick, and 15% because they thought they wouldn't work as well as other staff or other staff would not want to work with them. Nearly three-quarters (73%) of doctors would not seek professional help for mental health problems for fear of damaging their career (33%) or their professional reputation (30%), and because of the perceived stigma of having a mental health problem (20%).

Economic costs

The cost to employers of mental-health related sickness absence and staff turnover is estimated at £26 billion per year. Reduced productivity when working while unwell with a mental health condition costs an estimated 1.5 times as much as working time lost through sickness.

Public attitudes

Public attitudes to mental ill health are gradually improving, with less fear and more acceptance of people with mental health problems.

However, according to the annual national surveys of attitudes to mental illness in England:

⇨ one in eight people would not want to live next door to someone who has been mentally ill;

⇨ 20% of people think people with a history of mental illness should not hold public office (down from 22% in 2009);

⇨ 36% of people think someone with a mental health problem is prone to violence (up from 29% in 2003);

⇨ 57% believe people with mental health problems need to be kept in a psychiatric hospital (up from 52% in 2009);

⇨ 48% believe that someone with a mental health problem cannot be held responsible for their own actions (up from 45% in 2009);

⇨ only 66% believe residents 'have nothing to fear' from people coming into their neighbourhood to access mental health services – 34% do not – but 84% agree that no one has the right to exclude people with mental illness from their neighbourhood;

⇨ only 26% of people agree that most women who have been treated in hospital for mental illness can be trusted to babysit their child – 74% do not;

⇨ only 34% of people agree there should be less emphasis on protecting the public from people with mental illness – 66% do not;

⇨ only 59% agree that people with mental illness are far less of a danger than most people suppose – 41% do not;

⇨ only 75% (up from 66% in 2008) think that people with mental health problems should have the same rights to a job as anyone else (25% do not);

⇨ 15% (down from 18% in 2009) believe mental illness is caused by lack of self-discipline and will-power.

Direct social contact with people with mental health problems is the most effective way to challenge stigma and change public attitudes.

Media

77% of adults believe that the media does not do a good job in educating people about mental illness. Nearly four out of ten readers of national newspapers say they are the source of their beliefs about a link between mental illness and violence. About one in six readers affected by mental health problems say that newspaper portrayals of mental illness generally have discouraged them, or friends or relatives from seeking help for mental health problems. People with mental health problems are rarely quoted in articles about mental health issues – one survey of the British print media found they were only quoted in 6% of all pieces.

One survey of the British print media found that:

⇨ the criminal justice system (the police and the criminal courts) was the most common known source of stories about mental health;

⇨ messages about the risk of violence posed by people with mental health problems were present in 15% of stories, most of which implied the risk was high;

⇨ there was little coverage of mental health issues in either young people's media or black and Asian media;

⇨ people who had personal contact with people with mental health problems were more understanding of them, more critical of negative media reporting and more sceptical about links made by the media between mental health and violence;

⇨ journalists did not view mental health as a subject worthy of reporting in its own right.

⇨ Information from the National Mental Health Development Unit. Visit www.nmhdu.org.uk for more.

© The National Mental Health Development Unit

NATIONAL MENTAL HEALTH DEVELOPMENT UNIT

The reality of life with a mental health problem

A report by mental health charity Hafal, to be published this week, lifts the lid on the lives of people with serious mental illnesses.

By Madeleine Brindley

Each of the people who tell their stories in the *12 Lives* report reveal how they want to be treated as individuals and how services were often inconsistent. These are some of their experiences.

Colette Dawkin, who is a volunteer at Hafal, has bipolar disorder, which was triggered when she gave birth to her first child, Louise, when she was 18.

> **'At one point after my father's death I was psychotic, overspending, paranoid, crying all the time and unable to cope. When the manic period ended I became very depressed. I literally lay down on a settee for about five months'**

Although the illness has put a strain on her family life and relationships, she believes she is now in control.

Colette said: 'When I had my daughter, Louise, I had a difficult birth and nearly died. When I came out of hospital I was diagnosed with postnatal depression.

'I was prescribed Mogadon and Valium but I managed to wean myself off them by the time Louise was one. My life was OK again until I had my son four years later.

'The doctor said it was the sight of the babies that triggered my depression. It wasn't until 12 years later, when I was hospitalised after showing signs of mania as well as depression, that I was diagnosed with bipolar disorder.

'In 1986 I divorced my husband and lost my job as a refuge worker for Women's Aid. I had to move out of the house and sell the car. Then, after 18 months, I lost custody of my children.

'To help myself get back on my feet I attended a training course on helping people with learning disabilities. I began to feel I had conquered my illness and was quite well for the next few years.

'After five years my children came home to live with me. Everything was going well until four years ago when my father died of a heart attack.

'It initially made me manic and not depressed which was difficult for people, especially my mother, to understand.

'At one point after my father's death I was psychotic, overspending, paranoid, crying all the time and unable to cope. When the manic period ended I became very depressed. I literally lay down on a settee for about five months.

'I couldn't cook, shop or clean and I felt suicidal. I developed agoraphobia and was sectioned.

'At the time of my father's death I was living with my fiancé whom I'd been with for 18 months. He couldn't cope with my illness and eventually he visited the hospital and said he didn't want me back, so I became homeless as well.

'Bipolar is such a difficult illness because it affects your mood, personality and, in turn, your relationships. Looking back I really wish my husband and I could have had family therapy when our children were small.

'It was never explained to them why mammy was ill. My daughter used to say: "I'm angry, mam, not with you but with the illness." She was a tower of strength to me through the years.

'My son was affected differently. He couldn't accept it.

'I had 18 months of help from my community psychiatric nurse (CPN) but it was coming to Hafal that really helped me recover – up until then, in the 35 years I had bipolar, I was never offered psychological therapies, I only had medication.

'At Hafal, any time I need to talk I can. If I've got a problem I can either talk to the staff or I can talk to my peers. Within Hafal I feel totally accepted.

'I'm in control now. A few weeks ago my CPN said I no longer need help from her. And after some difficult times I've also got good relations with my children; I've built bridges with them and over the years they've come to understand my illness more.

'I really feel I've turned my illness on its head and that I'm giving something back for all the help I've received.'

Gulf war veteran Terry Taylor was diagnosed with bipolar disorder during his successful army career.

He said: 'I joined the army in 1989, the Gulf War started the following year and I went out as a combat engineer.

'I saw some terrible things but what affected me most was six months of isolation in the Gulf, being stuck with a bullying corporal who could make life difficult.

'The army can be a good cover-up for anyone who has depressive symptoms as the culture revolves around working hard and being rewarded in beer.

'Army life is full of high highs and low lows; it can be a melting pot for people with a mental disorder and drinking covers up a lot of it.

'Returning from the Gulf was an anti-climax. I went on leave from a frenetic job to nothing. To fill the gap I developed an artificial love of the rave scene. I started taking Ecstasy and became hooked.

'The police caught me with amphetamine but I wasn't thrown out of the army because I asked to see a psychiatrist; his report said I had substance-misuse disorder due to depression, that it wasn't in the public interest to prosecute me.

'The next tour was to Cyprus. Signs I had bipolar disorder (which runs in the family) were lurking through my army career but they hit home there.

'The weather became warmer – people with bipolar can get high when the weather warms up – and feelings of a religious nature welled up inside me. I was raised a Christian and though I never fully bought into it I felt that God was talking to me.

'I lost all my friends by the tour's end, I was too much to handle. When I'm high I can be extremely talkative and intense. I got hit by a low when I returned from Cyprus. I was not receiving any treatment then but fortunately, at least for me, Bosnia came up – if it hadn't I don't think I'd be here now.

'I was in Bosnia for six months. Although the work was very hard I was promoted and the camaraderie was great. At the tour's end I was very high, we had a long leave and I needed something to do so I went to Ireland for an adventure on a motorbike.

'I made it safely back to camp from Ireland though I was behaving strangely. Army officials should have realised I was ill then because I was wandering round the camp in the middle of the night cleaning things.

'Eventually I went to the town's cathedral thinking I was going to get married. I bought a £400 ring for a bride I was convinced was going to come. Eventually I sat at the back of the church and collapsed, crying. A priest found me, called the police and I was sent to Catterick Military Hospital.

'The hospital's psychiatrist told me I had bipolar disorder, I was hyper-manic and that on a scale of one to ten I was 15. The staff tried to give me medication but because of my memories of the rave scene, I thought taking pills was wrong, so I refused.

'After a few days five nurses waited until I was unaware and jumped me. Four held my limbs down, the fifth injected me. That was the worst moment of my life.

'The army accepted some responsibility for my illness and agreed the job made it worse. I was awarded £5,000 at a hearing.

'The army wanted me to stay but I left in 1997.

'Leaving was difficult as I missed the camaraderie.

'Since then, among other things, I've worked at an electrical company, backpacked around the US and I began an engineering apprenticeship.

'In all I've had six major psychotic episodes. I've noticed that in the media the word psychosis is rarely mentioned. It's as if it has become a bogey word used only on the rare occasions when somebody with a mental illness has hurt someone. Not using the word propagates fear and mistrust.

'In terms of my recovery I'm building myself up after last year's episode. For a 45-year-old I'm in good shape physically but mentally I can feel vulnerable and shaky.

'Playing sport has helped counter this, while visiting Hafal has eased my fears of becoming socially isolated. Playing my guitar has helped a lot – the discipline of playing music has been a huge help to me many times.

'I'm now involved in a community film project as a volunteer workshop leader helping people with learning difficulties, mental health issues and probation service users.'

11 October 2010

⇨ The above information is reprinted with kind permission from Wales Online. Visit www.walesonline. co.uk for more information.

© Media Wales Ltd.

Myths and facts about mental ill health

Information from Sussex Partnership NHS Foundation Trust.

Mental health problems are rare

This is a myth. Mental health problems affect one in four people in any one year. So, even if you don't have a mental health problem, it's likely your best friend, a family member or work colleague will be affected.

People with mental health problems are violent

This is a myth. People with mental health problems are much more likely to be the victim of violence. The violence myth makes it harder for people to talk openly about mental health problems. It can also make friends reluctant to stay in touch.

People can recover completely from a mental illness

This is a fact. Many people can and do recover completely from mental health problems. Alongside professional help, the support of friends and family and getting back to work are all important in helping people recover.

On average, people with severe mental illnesses die ten years younger

This is a fact. But it's not the mental illness that kills – it's the discrimination. The physical health needs of people with mental health problems are often dismissed, causing higher rates of death from heart attacks, diabetes and cancer for people with severe mental illness.

You can be open about mental health problems without fearing you'll be treated differently

This is a myth. People fear telling friends, family and work colleagues if they have a mental health problem because of stigma. In fact, 87% of people with a mental health problem have experienced discrimination.

There's not much you can do to help a friend experiencing a mental health problem

This is a myth. If someone you know is experiencing a mental health problem, just staying in touch can really help. For many people, it is the small things that friends do that can make a difference like visiting or phoning.

People can't work if they have a mental health problem

This is a myth. With one in four people affected by mental health problems, you probably work with someone with a mental health problem.

If you use a mental health service, there's a one in three chance you'll lose contact with friends

This is a fact. Sometimes friends feel like they don't know enough to be able to help, or feel uncomfortable. But you don't need to be an expert on mental health to be a friend. It's often the everyday things, like a phone call or text, that make a difference.

⇨ The above information is reprinted with kind permission from Sussex Partnership NHS Foundation Trust and the Time to Change Campaign. Visit http://sussexpartnership.demo.eibs.co.uk for more.

© Sussex Partnership NHS Foundation Trust and Time to Change Campaign

Fear of stigma stops employees with mental health problems from speaking out

Scores of British adults avoid talking to their boss about mental health problems out of fear of losing their job or being considered 'mad', new findings suggest.

A survey, published by mental health charity Rethink, shows that nearly six in ten British workers (59%) say they would feel uncomfortable talking to their line manager if they had a mental health condition such as depression, anxiety or bipolar disorder.

Fear of losing their job was the main reason people gave for feeling uncomfortable, closely followed by concern about colleagues finding out about their diagnosis. Nearly one in five (18%) respondents said they would be concerned that their line manager would think they were 'mad' or overlook them for promotion (17%).

Key findings:

⇨ 9% of British employees say they would feel 'very' comfortable talking to their line manager about a mental health condition, 24% say they would feel 'fairly' comfortable.

⇨ 27% would feel 'not very' comfortable and 32% 'not at all' comfortable.

⇨ More than a quarter (26%) of respondents who said they wouldn't feel comfortable talking to their line manager would be worried about losing their job.

⇨ Nearly one in five (18%) would worry that their line manager would think they were 'mad'.

⇨ 19% would be concerned that their colleagues would find out.

⇨ Others (16%) would be afraid they would be overlooked for promotion.

Antonia Borneo, Rethink's policy manager, said: 'These statistics confirm what our members tell us. Even when employers have mental health policies in place, line managers often feel ill-equipped to deal with mental health issues among staff. However, line managers have a huge role to play in tackling workplace stigma and helping people with mental illness to remain in work. We know the practical steps that can help people affected by mental illness to continue working and want to share this knowledge with employers so that all employees feel comfortable asking their manager for help.'

At a parliamentary event tomorrow (Thursday 4 March 2010), Rethink will launch a selection of guides for employees affected by mental illness and their line managers. These give advice about individuals' rights at work and list examples of reasonable adjustments available under the Disability Discrimination Act 1995. Reasonable adjustments can include flexible working hours, time off for treatment, and a phased return to work when necessary.

> *Nearly six in ten British workers (59%) say they would feel uncomfortable talking to their line manager if they had a mental health condition such as depression, anxiety or bipolar disorder*

Four years ago magazine journalist Josie Fletcher, 36, had a psychotic breakdown. She says:

'I was lucky enough to be given the time and space by my employers to recover properly before returning. I met with managers and HR, and a graduated return to work was planned, starting with one afternoon per week. This was built up over several months and my employers were patient. I now alternate five days a week in the office with four in the office and one working from home. Getting back to work was the final step in my recovery and one that boosted my confidence enormously. If I hadn't had a job to go back to, with familiar colleagues, I don't think I would have recovered as well.

'My advice to employers would be to try to understand that severe mental illness is as distressing as serious physical illness, just in a different way. A person's confidence will be at rock bottom but with the right support, time and space they can recover. Keeping hold of a valuable employee benefits the employer in the long term.'

11 March 2010

⇨ Information produced by the mental health charity Rethink, 2010. www.rethink.org

© Rethink

RETHINK

New intervention to reduce self-stigma among persons with serious mental illness

A new intervention has been found to reduce the self-stigma and improve the quality of life and self-esteem among persons with serious mental illness.

A new intervention, the result of a collaboration between researchers from the University of Haifa, City University of New York and Indiana University, was found to reduce the self-stigma and improve the quality of life and self-esteem among persons with serious mental illness.

'Just like wheelchairs and Braille have increased social integration for people with physical handicaps, there is also a need to identify and remove the barriers to community inclusion for people with serious mental illness,' says Professor Roe, Chair of the Department of Community Mental Health, Faculty of Social Welfare and Health Sciences at the University of Haifa who led the study together with his colleagues from the US – Professors Paul H. Lysaker from Indiana University School of Medicine, Department of Psychiatry, and Philip T. Yanos of the Department of Psychology, John Jay College of Criminal Justice, City University of New York, and from Israel – Dr Ilanit Hasson-Ohayon, Yaara Zisman-Ilani and Oren Deri.

Much attention has been given to making all facilities intended for the public accessible, in striving to gain equality for people with physical disabilities. But while the obstacles facing the physically challenged can be relatively easily identified, pinpointing the obstacles that persons with a mental illness must overcome is much harder.

According to Professor Roe, earlier studies have shown that one of the central obstacles is the negative stigma attached to mental illness by society at large, which is much more powerful than the labels attached to people with other disabilities. This stigma may lead to social exclusion. Another obstacle that may result from stigma is 'self-stigma', whereby people with a mental illness adopt and internalise the social stigma and experience loss of self-esteem and self-efficacy. 'People with a mental illness with elevated self-stigma report low self-esteem and low self-image, and as a result they refrain from taking an active role in various areas of life, such as employment, housing and social life,' Professor Roe explains.

In an attempt to address this problem, Professor Philip Yanos of City University of New York, Professor David Roe and Professor Paul Lysaker of Indiana University School of Medicine, with the help of a research grant from the National Institute of Mental Health, developed what they term 'Narrative Enhancement Cognitive Behavioral Therapy (NECT)', which is aimed at giving people with a mental illness the necessary tools to cope with the 'invisible' barrier to social inclusion – self-stigma.

The research team ran a 20-meeting pilot course of the new intervention at three separate locations: New York, Indiana and Israel. Following the pilot run, Professor Roe headed a study in Israel in which 21 people with a mental illness (with at least 40% mental handicap) completed the intervention. This study examined the effects of the intervention compared to a control group of 22 mentally ill people of similar disabilities who did not participate in the intervention. It showed that those who participated in the intervention exhibited a reduced self-stigma and, in parallel, an increase in quality of life and self-esteem.

'The intervention method that we developed helps persons with mental illness cope with one of the central obstacles that they face – self-stigma. We hope to be able to train more professionals in this intervention and root the method in rehabilitation centres and community health centres, so as to assist in recuperation processes and in community inclusion over a larger and more significant population of people with a mental illness,' Professor Roe concludes.
13 May 2010

⇨ The above information is reprinted with kind permission from the University of Haifa. Visit http://newmedia-eng.haifa.ac.il/?p=3052 to view this item on their website.

© *University of Haifa*

UNIVERSITY OF HAIFA

With rights in mind

Executive summary of a report from Youth Access.

⇨ Mental health problems are common among young people. At any one time, around one in six 16- to 24-year-olds meet thresholds for clinical diagnoses of problems such as anxiety and depression. When problems such as post traumatic stress, attempted suicide, eating disorders and alcohol and drug dependence are added in, the proportion affected rises to almost a third. Mental health problems are also common among the 11 to 16 age group, with around one in eight meeting thresholds for clinical diagnoses at any one time.

⇨ Mental health problems are much more common among certain groups of young people, such as those looked after by local authorities and those in custody.

⇨ Social welfare law problems are also known to be common among 18- to 24-year-olds. Around one in five report one or more such problems during a three-year period. More than one in three report wider civil law problems (including social welfare law problems). Some will almost certainly have been experienced at 16 or 17, and perhaps also at 15. But there is a gap in the evidence base regarding the full extent and nature of problems experienced by under-18s.

⇨ Evidence from the Civil and Social Justice Survey (CSJS) also suggests that both mental health problems, and social welfare and wider civil law problems, are more common among 18- to 24-year-olds who are not in education, employment or training (NEET) than those who are. Also, that stress-related illness, loss of confidence and worry, as a result of civil law problems generally, are more common among those who are NEET.

⇨ The full extent to which mental health problems may cause social welfare law problems and vice versa is hard to determine. But there is evidence that people with mental health problems are more likely than those without to experience a range of social welfare law and civil law problems. Also, that social welfare law and civil law problems can lead to and/or exacerbate stress and depression in particular, and can also have wider impacts on mental health, such as causing worry and loss of confidence.

⇨ The evidence base linking mental health problems and social welfare law problems tends to relate to adults generally. But there is also evidence indicating similar links among young people, both generally, and particularly with regard to homelessness and mental health.

⇨ In the CSJS, 15% of 18- to 24-year-olds who reported mental health problems (whether or not together with long-standing illness/disability) reported homelessness problems, compared to 1% of those reporting neither type of health problem. Approximately 35% who reported mental health problems reported housing problems more generally. This rose to approximately 50% among those who also reported long-standing illness or disability.

⇨ Looked at from the other direction, although the numbers involved were small, 62% of 18- to 24-year-olds in the CSJS who reported homelessness problems also reported mental health problems. In another survey, a third of 16- to 17-year-olds accepted as statutorily homeless reported current anxiety, depression or other mental health problems.

⇨ Notwithstanding the difficulties in establishing cause and effect, it seems clear that social welfare law advice should have a role to play in improving mental health, and in thus reducing the social and economic costs associated with mental ill health. Although as noted below, the evidence base for the impact of social welfare law advice is currently fairly limited, what evidence there is points to it potentially being instrumental to improvements in this area. And as Pleasence and Balmer (2009) put it:

To the extent that problems involving rights play a role in bringing about or exacerbating mental illness, there is a role for legal and advice services in its reduction... To the extent that mental illness plays a role in bringing about or exacerbating rights problems, advice services should be integrated with mental health services, to accommodate this and reflect the particular needs of people facing mental illness. To the extent that rights and mental health problems simply co-occur, advice and mental health services should anyway be integrated where possible, to enable clients/patients to receive 'seamless services'.

⇨ With regard to young people specifically, two other dimensions to mental health problems indicate the importance of advice that may help to ameliorate them. The first is that mental health problems experienced by children and young people are often enduring – and have been found to often persist three years after initial assessments. The second is that such problems are also frequently precursors to mental health problems later on in life. Both dimensions point up the importance of early intervention.

⇨ Several studies have sought to demonstrate impacts of advice quantitatively, using recognised measures of health. Some of these have compared mental health scores before and after advice. Some have also compared changes in mental health scores between clients who received advice and gained as a result, and those who did not. A small number of statistically significant improvements in mental health scores following advice have been noted, as have a small number of significantly greater improvements among those who gained as a result of advice, compared to those who did not.

⇨ Other quantitative studies, including two randomised controlled trials (RCTs), have not generated statistically significant findings of a similar nature. That, however, appears due to methodological limitations as much as anything else.

⇨ A number of studies have relied on self-reporting by clients (and sometimes their GPs). Whether quantitative or qualitative, these all point towards social welfare law advice being instrumental to improvements in mental health. In particular, reduced levels of stress and depression tend to be reported.

⇨ The evidence base here relates mainly to adults generally, but there is also some evidence regarding positive impacts of advice for young people aged 16 to 25, provided by YIACS (Youth Information, Advice, Counselling and Support Services).

⇨ There is scope for further research here. The evidence base is still fairly limited, and largely relates to impacts of welfare benefits advice accessed via healthcare settings and debt advice for adults generally. A need for further research into the impacts on mental health of advice for young people, and regarding homelessness and housing problems specifically, is indicated. Addressing the gap in the evidence base on the prevalence of social welfare and civil law problems among 16- to 17-year-olds would appear to be a useful preliminary step towards this.

⇨ Identifying and measuring impacts of social welfare law advice can, however, require considerable resources in terms of time and skills. Rigorous studies will be beyond most advice providers without substantial additional inputs.

⇨ Specific challenges relevant to researching the impact of advice on young people's mental health include establishing that tools used are age-appropriate, i.e. are capable of measuring aspects of mental health that are most relevant to them.

⇨ An additional consideration is that quite substantial proportions of people who report social welfare and civil law problems also report obtaining medical treatment, including counselling, for stress etc resulting from those problems. Isolating the effects

of social welfare law advice from the effects of such treatment can be a complex exercise. Improvements in emotional outlook may be attributed to practical help received from advice providers. But help from formal, non-legal sources that deal specifically with emotional or mental health difficulties may be equally important.

⇨ There is also evidence suggesting that people want help with debt problems to include counselling, 'someone to talk to and share feelings with', and 'help with stress and depression'. Research into the impact of social welfare law advice delivered in conjunction with counselling services, and which investigates what it is about each type of intervention that may be most beneficial for young people's mental health, would therefore seem of value.

⇨ Also, with regard to young people specifically, advice outcomes may be linked to the contexts in which it is received. Young people may prefer to get legal advice in youth settings, and favour either youth workers with good legal knowledge, or advisers/lawyers specialising in young people. This indicates a need for research on impacts to take account of young people's preferred methods of accessing advice.

January 2010

⇨ The above information is an extract from Youth Access' report *With rights in mind* by Mark Sefton, and is reprinted with permission. Visit www.youthaccess.org.uk for more information.

© Youth Access

YOUTH ACCESS

A manifesto for ending mental health stigma

The next government must repeal the law that stops me from standing for parliament – and take a look at my ideas for mental health.

By Clare Allan

A psychiatrist once told me that the fact I had been sectioned meant I was unable to stand for parliament. At the time, being unable to smoke was an issue of more immediate concern, but I do remember, even then, an awareness of something shifting inside me to fit this new information: I was not quite an adult any more. My status had changed. I would be forever less.

Under laws dating back to Elizabethan times, anyone who has been detained in a psychiatric hospital is banned from serving as an MP, even if he or she has made a full recovery. Section 141 of the Mental Health Act also forces MPs to give up their seats if they are sectioned for six months or more, regardless of the wishes of their constituents. No such stipulation applies to physical health; there is nothing legally to prevent an MP in a coma remaining an MP. It was this disparity and the stigmatising attitude it embodies that led the Speaker's Conference on parliamentary representation to recommend in January that section 141 should be repealed. It is to be hoped that any new government will act swiftly on this recommendation. As recently as 2007, MPs considered section 141 and shockingly elected to retain it.

It is the stigma surrounding mental health problems often far more than the problems themselves that holds people back and prevents them from becoming full and active members of society. Not only is this bad for the mental health of the individuals concerned, it is also a terrible waste of the talents and experience these people have to offer society.

Stigma derives from deeply ingrained individual and social attitudes, and these take time, courage and determination to change. For any government committed to the task, the places where stigma is enshrined in law would seem an obvious place to start. It is therefore immensely regrettable that, despite repeated promises since 2004 to consult on the issue, the Ministry of Justice announced in January that it would not now be holding a consultation on the law preventing those with mental health problems from serving on a jury. No explanation has been offered.

But an amendment to the equality bill, which was due to be debated in the Commons yesterday, offers real hope of positive change. Provided they can get it through in time – and they are certainly taking it down to the wire – the law, which will prohibit prospective employers from asking applicants about their health history until after the offer of a job has been made, will be the single best thing this government has done for the prospects of those who have experienced mental health problems.

Perhaps the next government will finally repeal that 450-year-old common law that prevents me from standing for parliament. In the meantime, these are my mental health election pledges, made secure in the knowledge that I will not be required to find a way to bring them about.

Under laws dating back to Elizabethan times, anyone who has been detained in a psychiatric hospital is banned from serving as an MP

First, there will be a massive investment in the welfare and wellbeing of children. Every school will have a counselling service and every estate will have a youth centre and dedicated youth workers. Class sizes will be halved and the increasingly narrow vocational focus of education will be reversed. Education is about developing the potential and confidence of each individual child, not programming a workforce.

Second, the benefits system will be completely overhauled. Those with long-term health problems will be able to enter education and work while remaining on full benefits for a period of three years.

Everyone will have access to a full range of mental health services, including talking therapies. What is available will no longer depend on where someone lives, and that includes prisons.

The physical health of those with mental health problems will be urgently addressed. On average, people with mental illness die ten years earlier than the rest of the population.

Carers will be given a salary, proper support and full holiday entitlement. Young carers will be given their own support worker dedicated to looking after their welfare.

That's just a start, and already I hear the bean-counters protesting. But mental illness already costs us £77 billion each year. In the long run, these measures could save us money. What they could save us in human terms is immeasurable.

7 April 2010

THE GUARDIAN

How to improve your mental wellbeing

This article explains what keeps people mentally well, why some people may be more prone to mental distress, and what you can do to promote your mental wellbeing. It also tells you how to support someone else in distress.

What do we mean by good mental health?

Good mental health isn't something you have, but something you do. To be mentally healthy you must value and accept yourself. This means that:

⇨ You care about yourself and you care for yourself. You love yourself, not hate yourself. You look after your physical health – eat well, sleep well, exercise and enjoy yourself.

⇨ You see yourself as being a valuable person in your own right. You don't have to earn the right to exist. You exist, so you have the right to exist.

⇨ You judge yourself on reasonable standards. You don't set yourself impossible goals, such as 'I have to be perfect in everything I do', and then punish yourself when you don't reach those goals.

Good mental health isn't something you have, but something you do. To be mentally healthy you must value and accept yourself

If you don't value and accept yourself, you are always frightened that other people will reject you. To prevent people seeing how unacceptable you are, you keep them at a distance, and so you are always frightened and lonely. If you value yourself, you don't expect people to reject you. You aren't frightened of other people. You can be open, and so you enjoy good relationships.

If you value and accept yourself, you are able to relax and enjoy yourself without feeling guilty. When you face a crisis, you know that, no matter how difficult the situation is, you will manage. How we see ourselves is central to every decision we make. People who value and accept themselves cope with life.

Why do some people become mentally distressed when others don't?

All of us grow up with a set of ideas about who we are, what our life was and will be, and what the world is like. These ideas come from our past experience, and, because no two people ever have the same experience, no two people ever see things in exactly the same way.

Our ideas aren't an exact picture of what's going on around us, but a set of guesses or theories about what's going on. If we grow up with certain views or beliefs about how life is or should be we can then be greatly shocked if we discover that things aren't the way we thought they were and that we've made a serious error of judgement.

Whenever we encounter some unexpected disaster or setback, we discover that there's a serious discrepancy between what we thought our life was and what it actually is. Perhaps we thought our life was safe and secure, and then we suffered a terrorist attack. Perhaps we thought we were going to spend the rest of our life with one special person, and then that person left us, or died. Perhaps we'd grown up believing that if we were good, nothing bad would happen to us, and then something did.

Whenever we discover we've made a serious error of judgement, we may start to doubt every judgement we've ever made. Then we start to feel very unsure of ourselves.

If we value and accept ourselves, we have confidence in ourselves, and, even though we're frightened, we tell ourselves that this feeling will pass, that we'll be able to meet the challenge and cope with whatever follows. If we don't value and feel positive about ourselves in this way, we may feel that we're about to break down, and so we have to find some defence to hold ourselves together. The less good we feel about ourselves, the more desperate the defence we resort to.

These defences might include:

⇨ harming our body by injuring it or by starving it;

MIND

- ⇨ blaming ourselves for the disaster or setback, and so becoming depressed;

- ⇨ locating the cause of our fear in the world around us and becoming too frightened to venture out;

- ⇨ getting busier and busier to avoid thinking about any problems;

- ⇨ trying to make everything secure by obsessively cleaning and checking;

- ⇨ retreating into our own inner world and giving up trying to make sense of the world around us in the way other people do.

We don't consciously choose a particular defence. Instead, we unconsciously and quickly resort to the one defence available to us because of the way we see ourselves and our world. For instance, if you are well-practised in blaming yourself for everything that goes wrong, you'll blame yourself for any crisis or bad luck you have.

Why is attitude so important?

Mental distress is not compulsory. However, if we don't value and accept ourselves, we're making sure that we will feel mental distress when life is difficult. If we do feel positive about ourselves, then when we suffer loss, we feel sad, not depressed. So, when someone treats us badly, we feel angry, but not guilty because we feel angry. When someone or something threatens us, we feel frightened, but we're not overwhelmed, because we look after ourselves and make ourselves safe.

What causes us to become mentally distressed is not loss, or poverty, or sickness, or people treating us badly. It's how we interpret our loss, or poverty, or sickness, or the fact that people are treating us badly.

Many people defeat themselves by interpreting what happens to them in a way that makes suffering inevitable. If we see ourselves as being bad and unacceptable, and we believe that we live in a 'just world' where goodness is rewarded and badness punished, then, when we suffer a disaster or setback, we interpret the event as being the punishment for our wickedness. If we see ourselves as being insignificant and worthless then, when the chance for happiness comes along, we say to ourselves, 'I wasn't meant to be happy'. If we are frightened of other people, when other people treat us badly we feel we've no right to stand up for ourselves.

If we desperately need other people around us, but see ourselves as unattractive and unlovable, we bury our anger. We let other people walk all over us, because we dare not show our displeasure in case other people reject us. If we believe that it's inevitable that other people will let us down and everything turn out badly, we'll not do anything to improve our life. So we suffer.

Isn't it all genetic?

Some people like to blame their genes or their fate for their misery, because then it seems that they're not responsible for what has happened to them. Many doctors like to blame some undiscovered gene or biochemical change for their patients' misery. This is because such doctors feel more comfortable with medical interpretations of events than with psychological interpretations. However, genes are very much affected by the environment, and despite the huge amount of time, money and effort that has been spent in the search for the genes that directly cause mental disorders, none have been discovered.

Serotonin levels

Changes in the levels of the chemicals (neurotransmitters) serotonin and noradrenaline have been found in the brains of people who are depressed – but not always. The biochemical changes that are associated with depression may be the result of the mood change rather than the cause of it, and no biochemical change has been found to precede the onset of depression. It is not correct to say that depression is caused by a chemical imbalance in the brain.

Genetics

It's often claimed that research shows depression runs in families and is therefore genetically inherited. But analysis of this research still leaves this open to question. We usually inherit a lot about our environment from our parents as well as our genes. Much of what we get from our parents is through learning. We can learn, from our family, ways of thinking that lead to distress. If a parent is constantly frightened and pessimistic, their child is likely to grow up believing that the world is a terrible place, and so the child becomes frightened and pessimistic.

What can I do about it?

Accept that you can change. Nobody stays the same, so you may as well change for the better. The big change that you need to make is to come to value and accept yourself. If you've spent most of your life believing that you're unacceptable and of little value, it's hard to change, because all your ideas and ways of behaving are based on that assumption.

The trick is to say to yourself, 'I don't think much of myself, but from now on I'm going to act as if I'm my own best friend. I'm going to be kind to myself, look after myself, and stop criticising myself and putting myself down'. Acting as if you're your own best friend will lead you to become that.

You need to be very aware of how you talk to yourself. Listen to the voice in your head. Write down the hurtful, critical things that voice says to you, and then think of better, kinder, more encouraging things to say to yourself.

For instance, when you have to do something, if you always say to yourself, 'You're sure to fail. You always make a mess of everything you do', write that down, and then beside it put, 'You're going to do the best you possibly can. It doesn't matter if you don't get it perfectly right, because the good thing about mistakes is that you learn from them'. Practise saying encouraging things to yourself.

Question the assumptions on which you base your ideas. Is it really true that everybody in the whole world hates you, or that everything you've ever done has turned out badly? Is it really true that every unfortunate thing that happens to you is your punishment for being such a wicked person? Look at the consequences of your ideas. If you don't get close to anyone because you fear being rejected, doesn't it follow that you will always be lonely?

If you think of yourself as bad try to remember how you came to think of yourself that way. Is this what your parents or spouse always told you? Were you really bad, or were they taking their bad feelings out on you?

Writing these things down puts what you're thinking and feeling outside of yourself, and you can see it more clearly.

Talk it through

Talk about these things to other people and find out how they see things. Talk to friends, call at a local drop-in centre, join a self-help group.

Talking to a therapist or counsellor can be very helpful. There are many different kinds of therapies, but they all

fall into one of two groups. There are prescriptive therapies and exploratory therapies. Prescriptive therapies, such as cognitive therapy, teach skills to overcome specific problems. Exploratory therapies, such as psychotherapy, explore your ideas and your experiences. Most therapists and counsellors use a bit of both.

Finding a therapist or counsellor can be difficult. Ask your GP whether there's a counsellor at their practice or whether she or he can refer you to an NHS psychologist or psychotherapist. See what your local Mind association has to offer. Look through the registers of psychotherapists and counsellors at your local library or on the Internet. The fact that a psychotherapist's or counsellor's name is on a register isn't a guarantee that the person is an effective psychotherapist or counsellor. But it does mean that if something goes wrong, you can complain to that person's professional organisation. No therapist or counsellor can wave a magic wand and make you better, but they can act as a guide on your journey of self-discovery.

What can I do about the things I can't change?

Remember, it's not what happens to us that causes our distress, but how we interpret what happens to us.

For example, if your mother always belittles and hurts you, and if you believe you have to visit her every week, then you make sure that you suffer.

If you decide that it isn't strictly necessary to see her every week and it's your responsibility to look after yourself, then you can control how often and for how long you see her. You'll create an emotional distance between yourself and her by seeing her not as your mother, but as a woman who prefers the immediate satisfaction of taking her bad feelings out on someone to the long-term satisfaction of having a loving child who wants to be with her.

This is what you need to do with all the things in your life that you can't change: find an interpretation of events that you can live with. Don't let these things dominate your life, taking up all your time and effort.

Even when life is at its most difficult, make sure that, every day, you give yourself something nice. This could be a treat, or time to do nothing but rest, chat with a friend, look at nature, or listen to music. Even if nobody else is looking after you, you can look after yourself. (See Mind's booklet *How to look after yourself.*)

⇨ The above information is reprinted from the Mind factsheet *How to improve your mental wellbeing* © Mind 2008. Visit www.mind.org.uk for more information on a wide range of mental health topics.

© Mind 2008

Mental health: strengthening our response

Information from WHO.

> ## Key facts
>
> ⇨ More than 450 million people suffer from mental disorders. Many more have mental problems.
>
> ⇨ Mental health is an integral part of health; indeed, there is no health without mental health.
>
> ⇨ Mental health is more than the absence of mental disorders.
>
> ⇨ Mental health is determined by socio-economic, biological and environmental factors.
>
> ⇨ Cost-effective intersectoral strategies and interventions exist to promote mental health.

Mental health is an integral and essential component of health. The WHO constitution states: 'Health is a state of complete physical, mental and social wellbeing and not merely the absence of disease or infirmity.' An important consequence of this definition is that mental health is described as more than the absence of mental disorders or disabilities.

Mental health is a state of wellbeing in which an individual realises his or her own abilities, can cope with the normal stresses of life, can work productively and is able to make a contribution to his or her community. In this positive sense, mental health is the foundation for individual wellbeing and the effective functioning of a community.

Determinants of mental health

Multiple social, psychological, and biological factors determine the level of mental health of a person at any point in time. For example, persistent socio-economic pressures are recognised risks to mental health for individuals and communities. The clearest evidence is associated with indicators of poverty, including low levels of education.

Poor mental health is also associated with rapid social change, stressful work conditions, gender discrimination, social exclusion, unhealthy lifestyle, risks of violence and physical ill-health and human rights violations.

There are also specific psychological and personality factors that make people vulnerable to mental disorders. Lastly, there are some biological causes of mental disorders, including genetic factors and imbalances in chemicals in the brain.

Strategies and interventions

Mental health promotion involves actions to create living conditions and environments that support mental health and allow people to adopt and maintain healthy lifestyles. These include a range of actions to increase the chances of more people experiencing better mental health.

A climate that respects and protects basic civil, political, socio-economic and cultural rights is fundamental to mental health promotion. Without the security and freedom provided by these rights, it is very difficult to maintain a high level of mental health.

National mental health policies should not be solely concerned with mental disorders, but should also recognise and address the broader issues which promote mental health. This includes mainstreaming mental health promotion into policies and programmes in government and business sectors including education, labour, justice, transport, environment, housing and welfare, as well as the health sector.

Promoting mental health depends largely on intersectoral strategies. Specific ways to promote mental health include:

⇨ early childhood interventions (e.g. home visits for pregnant women, pre-school psycho-social activities, combined nutritional and psycho-social help for disadvantaged populations);

⇨ support to children (e.g. skills-building programmes, child and youth development programmes);

⇨ socio-economic empowerment of women (e.g. improving access to education and microcredit schemes);

⇨ social support for elderly populations (e.g. befriending initiatives, community and day centres for the aged);

⇨ programmes targeted at vulnerable groups, including minorities, indigenous people, migrants and people affected by conflicts and disasters (e.g. psycho-social interventions after disasters);

⇨ mental health promotional activities in schools (e.g. programmes supporting ecological changes in schools and child-friendly schools);

⇨ mental health interventions at work (e.g. stress prevention programmes);

⇨ housing policies (e.g. housing improvement);

⇨ violence prevention programmes (e.g. community policing initiatives); and

⇨ community development programmes (e.g. 'Communities That Care' initiatives, integrated rural development).

WORLD HEALTH ORGANIZATION

WHO response

WHO supports governments in the goal of strengthening and promoting mental health. WHO has evaluated evidence for promoting mental health and is working with governments to disseminate this information and to integrate the effective strategies into policies and plans.

More specifically, WHO's mental health Gap Action Programme (mhGAP) aims at scaling up services for mental, neurological and substance use disorders for countries, especially with low and middle incomes.

When adopted and implemented, tens of millions can be treated for depression, schizophrenia and epilepsy, be prevented from suicide and can begin to lead normal lives – even where resources are scarce.

September 2010
Accessed November 2010. Fact sheet N°220. http://www. who.int/mediacentre/factsheets/fs220/en/index.html

⇨ Information from the World Health Organization. Visit www.who.int for more.

© *World Health Organization*

Young people could fall through mental health care 'gap'

Many young people with mental health problems are at risk of falling through a huge gap in provision when they move from adolescent to adult care services, according to new research from the University of Warwick.

A team led by Professor Swaran Singh at Warwick Medical School looked at the transition from child mental health services to adult mental health services and found for the vast majority of users the move was 'poorly planned, poorly executed and poorly experienced'.

In a study published in *The British Journal of Psychiatry*, the research team looked at 154 service users who were crossing the boundary from child to adult mental health services. They followed the sample group for one year to examine their experiences.

Of the cohort of 154, only 58% made the transition to adult mental health services. The researchers found that individuals with a history of severe mental illness, being on medication or having been admitted to hospital were more likely to make a transition than those with neurodevelopmental disorders, emotional/ neurotic disorders and emerging personality disorder. The research team also found that a fifth of all actual referrals that crossed the boundary to adult mental health services in this study were discharged without being seen.

Professor Singh said: 'Despite adolescence being a risk period for the emergence of serious mental disorders, substance misuse, other risk-taking behaviours and poor engagement with health services, mental health provision is often patchy during this period. By following a paediatric-adult split, mental health services introduce discontinuities in care provision where the system should be most robust. Often for the vast majority the transition from child to adult mental health services is poorly planned, poorly executed and poorly experienced.'

The team found that information transfer between child and adult mental health services was hampered by a lack of understanding of each other's services, inconsistent documentation, different systems used for transfer of electronic information and transfer of referrals to lengthy waiting lists during which time dialogue between mental health professionals on each side was reduced.

Professor Singh added: 'Where possible case notes should follow the young person and detailed referral letters, including risk assessments, should be sent to adult mental health services to facilitate planning. We need to ensure that the vital need for improving youth mental health is not ignored for fear of dismantling long-standing and yet unhelpful service barriers.'

12 October 2010

⇨ The above information is reprinted with kind permission from the University of Warwick. Visit www. warwick.ac.uk for more information.

© *University of Warwick*

Only one in six people with mental illness receives recommended treatment

New research from mental health charity Rethink has revealed a desperate need for improvements within the NHS to ensure that people experiencing mental illness receive the necessary care and treatment.

The charity, which has launched a major new campaign, Fair Treatment Now, says that billions of pounds are being wasted each year on ineffective mental health services.

A Rethink poll of more than 400 people who use mental health services showed that the majority are regularly missing out on the treatment they are entitled to – and should receive – according to guidance from the National Institute for Health and Clinical Excellence (NICE).

The poll found that:

⇨ Just one in six (16%) service users receive all the treatments recommended by NICE.

⇨ Fewer than half of people with schizophrenia and bipolar disorder are being offered psychological therapies, as recommended.

⇨ Only one in three (32%) mental health service users have been offered a physical health check, even though people with severe mental illness are likely to die ten years younger than other citizens, often from preventable physical illnesses.

⇨ Fewer than half (47%) have been offered information about the side effects of medication, even when side effects present significant health risks, such as diabetes and rapid weight gain.

A second Rethink poll, this time of 251 general practitioners, found that doctors themselves have a negative view of mental health services.

⇨ Only half of GPs (50%) are confident about the quality of specialist care for depression, compared with more than nine in ten (95%) who are confident about treatment for cardiovascular disease.

⇨ Only 1% of GPs are 'very confident' that a patient with psychosis will not come to harm while they wait for their treatment assessment.

⇨ Fewer than a third (29%) think that a patient with psychosis will be supported to recover long-term. Just one-third are confident in the quality of care on offer to people with psychosis.

Paul Jenkins, Rethink's chief executive, said: 'For too long, people with severe mental illnesses such as schizophrenia have been denied the treatments that they need.

'It is critical that action is taken to bring mental health services up to the same standard as those available for other illnesses.

'Mental illness costs us all around £33.75 billion each year, but less than a quarter of this is spent on providing good quality care. Most of it is channelled into other public services which are needed to pick up the consequences of failing to provide early, effective treatment.

'It doesn't have to be like this – we know that the right treatment from the outset can save millions in the long run. It is paramount that appropriate action is taken to improve the lives of the more than 1.5 million people affected by severe mental illness.'

Rethink, the leading charity delivering services and campaigning in the field of severe mental illness, wants to see:

⇨ Improved access to psychological therapies for people affected by severe mental illness (for people with schizophrenia, talking therapy can save £1,000 per person).

⇨ More effective outcome targets in order to better record and assess the quality of services.

⇨ Payment by Results for NHS staff to be extended to mental health services.

⇨ The NHS Choose and Book system to be available for people with mental illness so that they can select who treats them.

⇨ The new, independent patients' body, Healthwatch, to focus on the needs of people with enduring conditions such as severe mental illness.

16 July 2010

⇨ The above information is reprinted with kind permission from Rethink. Visit their website at www.rethink.org for more information on this and other related topics.

© Rethink

RETHINK

The Mental Health Act

The Mental Health Act 1983 covers the assessment, treatment and rights of people with a mental health condition.

Assessment and treatment

Many people receive specialist mental health care and treatment in the community. Some people can experience severe mental health problems that require admission to hospital for assessment and treatment.

People can only be detained if the strict criteria laid down in the Act are met. The person must be suffering from a mental disorder as defined by the Act.

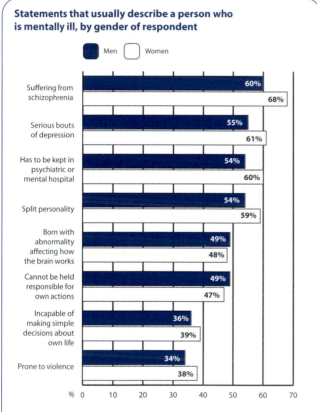

Statements that usually describe a person who is mentally ill, by gender of respondent

- Men
- Women

Statement	Men	Women
Suffering from schizophrenia	60%	68%
Serious bouts of depression	55%	61%
Has to be kept in psychiatric or mental hospital	54%	60%
Split personality	54%	59%
Born with abnormality affecting how the brain works	49%	48%
Cannot be held responsible for own actions	49%	47%
Incapable of making simple decisions about own life	36%	39%
Prone to violence	34%	38%

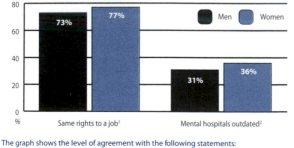

Attitudes towards integrating people with mental illness into community, by gender of respondent

- Men
- Women

	Men	Women
Same rights to a job[1]	73%	77%
Mental hospitals outdated[2]	31%	36%

The graph shows the level of agreement with the following statements:
[1] People with mental health problems should have the same rights to a job as anyone else.
[2] Mental hospitals are an outdated means of treating people with mental illness.

Source: Attitudes to mental illness 2010 research report, March 2010,
© The Department of Health-funded anti-stigma programme, Crown Copyright

An application for assessment or treatment must be supported in writing by two registered medical practitioners. The recommendation must include a statement about why an assessment and/or treatment is necessary, and why other methods of dealing with the patient are not appropriate.

Admissions to hospital

Most people who receive treatment in hospitals or psychiatric units for mental health conditions are there on a voluntary basis and have the same rights as people receiving treatment for physical illnesses.

However, a small number of patients may need to be compulsorily detained under a section of the Mental Health Act.

The nearest relative's power of discharge can be overruled by the doctor who is responsible for the patient's treatment. The doctor can only do this if they think the patient is likely to act dangerously if discharged

The Act explains who is involved in the decision about compulsory admission or detention, and the individual's or their nearest relative's right of appeal.

Approved mental health professional

An approved mental health professional is a mental health worker who has received special training. They can provide help and give assistance to people who are being treated under the Mental Health Act. They can be community psychiatric nurses, occupational therapists, social workers or psychologists. Their functions can include helping to assess whether a person needs to be compulsorily detained (sectioned) as part of their treatment.

They are also responsible for ensuring that the human and civil rights of a person being detained under the Mental Health Act are respected and upheld.

Nearest relative

The Act gives certain rights to the nearest relative which can be used to protect the patient's interests.

Usually, the nearest relative is the person who occurs highest in the following list:

⇨ husband, wife or civil partner;

⇨ partner (of either sex) who has lived with the patient for at least six months;

⇨ daughter or son;

⇨ father or mother;

⇨ brother or sister;

⇨ grandfather or grandmother;

⇨ aunt or uncle;

⇨ nephew or niece.

If a person from the list above lives with or cares for the patient, that person is likely to be regarded as the nearest relative. A person who is not a relative but who has lived with the patient for at least five years can also be regarded as the nearest relative.

The appointment of the nearest relative can only be changed by a County Court.

What the nearest relative can do

The nearest relative has the right to:

⇨ apply for compulsory assessment or treatment of the patient, or ask social services to ask an approved mental health worker to consider the patient's case

⇨ be told if an approved mental health worker applies for the patient to be detained for compulsory assessment;

⇨ be consulted about, and object to, an approved mental health worker applying for the patient to be detained for compulsory treatment;

⇨ apply to a Mental Health Tribunal on behalf of the patient in certain situations;

⇨ receive written information about the patient's detention, rights and discharge unless the patient objects;

⇨ discharge the patient.

The nearest relative's power of discharge can be overruled by the doctor who is responsible for the patient's treatment. The doctor can only do this if they think the patient is likely to act dangerously if discharged.

Finding out more about the Mental Health Act 1983

The most common sections of the Act under which patients are compulsorily admitted to a hospital are:

⇨ section 2: admission to hospital for up to 28 days for assessment;

⇨ section 3: admission to hospital for up to six months for treatment;

⇨ section 4: admission on an emergency basis for up to 72 hours.

The mental health charity Mind have an outline guide to the Mental Health Act on their website (www.mind. org.uk).

Further information and guidance about the Mental Health Act can also be found on the Department of Health website (www.dh.gov.uk).

⇨ Information from Directgov. Visit www.direct.gov. uk for more.

DIRECTGOV

KEY FACTS

⇨ The cost of mental ill health in England is now £105.2 billion a year, according to an update published by the Centre for Mental Health. (page 1)

⇨ Some children and young people live with a parent who has a serious mental illness, such as depression, personality disorder or schizophrenia. The child may be affected by their parent's often reduced capacity to cope as a parent, and also by the parent's illness directly. (page 4)

⇨ Mental health problems are very common. Estimates from research studies suggest that one in four people in the UK experiences a diagnosable mental health problem at some point during their life. (page 5)

⇨ Six out of ten of people (62%) in Great Britain (71% of women and 52% of men) have had at least one time in their life where they have found it difficult to cope mentally, according to the results of an online YouGov poll released by the mental health charity Together. (page 6)

⇨ Healthy young adults sleeping less than five hours a night are three times more likely to develop mental ill health than those sleeping eight to nine hours, according to a new study. (page 7)

⇨ Of the UK's 175,000 young carers, over 50,000 – 29% – are estimated to care for a family member with mental health problems. (page 8)

⇨ A 17-year study of nearly 1,000 elderly people found that 22% of those who were depressed at the start went on to develop dementia compared with 17% of those who were not depressed, BBC News reported. (page 12)

⇨ About one in every 100 people will have schizophrenia at some time in their lives. People with schizophrenia often also have depression, anxiety or a personality disorder. Between five and ten per cent will take their own lives. (page 16)

⇨ One US study has found that 50% of people with mental health problems were also abusing drugs or alcohol at a problematic level. Very little research has been conducted in the UK: however, it is a very real problem here. (page 17)

⇨ During the First World War, Post Traumatic Stress Disorder was referred to as 'shell shock'; as 'war neurosis' during WWII, and as 'combat stress reaction' during the Vietnam War. In the 1980s the term Post Traumatic Stress Disorder was introduced – the term we still use today. (page 20)

⇨ People with severe mental health problems have a lower rate of employment than any other disabled group but they are more likely than any other group with disabilities to want to have a job. (page 22)

⇨ Only 66% believe residents 'have nothing to fear' from people coming into their neighbourhood to access mental health services – 34% do not – but 84% agree that no one has the right to exclude people with mental illness from their neighbourhood. (page 23)

⇨ It is a myth that people with mental health problems are usually violent. Actually, people with mental health problems are much more likely to be the victim of violence. (page 26)

⇨ Mental health problems are much more common among certain groups of young people, such as those looked after by local authorities and those in custody. (page 29)

⇨ Mental health is determined by socio-economic, biological and environmental factors. (page 35)

⇨ A Rethink poll of more than 400 people who use mental health services showed that the majority are regularly missing out on the treatment they are entitled to. (page 37)

⇨ The Mental Health Act 1983 covers the assessment, treatment and rights of people with a mental health condition. (page 38)

Alzheimer's disease

A progressive form of dementia involving deterioration of the brain tissue. Alzheimer's patients suffer from memory loss, confusion, mood swings and personality changes. Most often, it is diagnosed in elderly people, although the rarer early-onset Alzheimer's can occur much earlier. Alzheimer's disease is a terminal illness for which there is no cure.

Antidepressants

These include tricyclic antidepressants (TCAs), selective serotonin re-uptake inhibitors (SSRIs) and monoamine oxidase inhibitors (MAOIs). Antidepressants work by boosting one or more chemicals (neurotransmitters) in the nervous system, which may be present in insufficient amounts during a depressive illness.

Anxiety

Anxiety can be described as a feeling of fear, apprehension, tension and/or stress. Most people experience anxiety from time to time and this is a perfectly normal response to stress. However, some individuals suffer from anxiety disorders which cause them to experience symptoms such as intense, persistent fear or nervousness, panic attacks and hyperventilation.

Bereavement

The loss of a loved one through death. Grief following a bereavement can be the trigger for or contribute to a mental illness in some cases, as can other traumatic life events such as being the victim of abuse or violence; divorce/separation; bullying, or being unable to cope financially.

Bipolar disorder

Previously called manic depression, this illness is characterised by mood swings where periods of severe depression are balanced by periods of elation and overactivity (mania).

Cognitive behavioural therapy (CBT)

A psychological treatment which assumes that behavioural and emotional reactions are learned over a long period. A cognitive therapist will seek to identify the source of emotional problems and develop techniques to overcome them.

Dementia

Mental deterioration and a reduction in brain function caused by loss of brain cells. Alzheimer's disease is the most common form of dementia.

Depression

Someone is said to be significantly depressed, or suffering from depression, when feelings of sadness or misery don't go away quickly and are so bad that they interfere with everyday life. Symptoms can also include low self-esteem and a lack of motivation.

Dual diagnosis

People who are diagnosed as having problematic substance abuse and a serious mental illness.

Post-Traumatic Stress Disorder (PTSD)

PTSD is a psychological response to an intensely traumatic event. It is commonly observed in members of the armed forces and has been known by different names at different times in history: during the First World War, for example, it was known as 'shell shock'.

Psychiatrist

A medical doctor who specialises in diagnosing and treating mental disorders. This is different from a psychologist, who is a professional or academic (not necessarily a doctor) specialising in understanding the human mind, thought and human behaviour.

Psychosis

A mental state in which the perception of reality is distorted.

Schizophrenia

Disorder characterised by hallucinations, paranoid delusions and abnormal thought patterns.

abuse, effects on children 3
alcohol abuse and mental illness 17
alcohol-related brain impairment 10
approved mental health professionals 38
asylum seekers, young 2
attitude and mental health 33
avoidance symptoms, Post Traumatic Stress Disorder 21

bereavement, effects on children 2
bipolar disorder 14–15, 24–5
black young people, mental health problems 2
bullying, effects on young people 2

cared-for children, and mental health problems 3–4
carers, young, and mental health problems 4
children and mental health problems 2–4
costs
  of mental health care 5
  of mental ill health 1, 23
crime and mental health sufferers 22
cyclothymic disorder 15

death
  earlier death of mental health sufferers 26
  effect of bereavement on children 2
dementia
  and depression 12–13
  and younger people 10–11
dementia services
  costs 5
  and younger people 10–11
depression and dementia 12–13
determinants of mental health 35
diagnosis
  bipolar disorder 15
  dementia in younger people 10
disability and mental health, young people 3
discrimination, racial 2
divorce, effects on children 3
domestic violence, effects on children 3
driving, dementia sufferers 11
dual diagnosis 9, 17

early onset dementia 10–11
emotional abuse, effects on children 3
employment and mental health sufferers 22–3, 27
  dementia sufferers 11
Equality Bill 31
ethnic minority young people, mental health problems 2

fronto-temporal lobar degeneration (FTLD) 10

gay and lesbian young people, mental health problems 3
genetics and mental health 33
good mental health 32
government, mental health strategy 5
guilt and Post Traumatic Stress Disorder 21

housing problems, young mental health sufferers 29
hyper-arousal symptoms, Post Traumatic Stress Disorder 21

investment in mental health services 5
isolation 6

lesbian and gay young people, mental health problems 3

manic-depressive illness (bipolar disorder) 14–15, 24–5
media and mental ill health 23
mental health
  definition 32, 35
  improving 33–4, 35–6
Mental Health Act 38–9
mental health problems
  causes 32–3
  children and young people 2–4
  costs 1, 5, 23
  prevalence 5, 6
  and social welfare law problems 29
mental health services 5
  insufficiencies 37
  and young people 10–11, 36
mental health stigma see stigma
mental health strategies 5, 35

parents
  with mental health problems, effects on children 4, 8–9
  in prison, effect on children 4
  separation, effects on children 3
physical health problems and schizophrenia 16–17
Pick's disease 10
Post Traumatic Stress Disorder (PTSD) 20–21
poverty and mental health problems 4
prevalence of mental health problems 5, 6
prison and mental health, young people 4
psychosis 18–19
PTSD (Post Traumatic Stress Disorder) 20–21
public attitudes to mental ill health 23

racism, effects on young people 2
rapid-cycling bipolar disorder 15
re-experiencing symptoms, Post Traumatic Stress Disorder 20
refugees, young 2

schizophrenia 16–17
self-stigma 28
serotonin levels and mental health 33
sexual abuse, effects on children 3
sleep deprivation, young people 7
social welfare law problems, young people 29–30
stigma
  mental health sufferers 22–3, 31
  self-stigma 28
  young carers 8
symptoms

Post Traumatic Stress Disorder 20–21
psychosis 18
schizophrenia 16

therapies 34
treatment
    bipolar disorder 15
    psychosis 18–19
    statistics 37

vascular dementia 10
victimisation of mental health sufferers 22

violence and mental ill health 22, 26

work *see* employment
working age dementia 10–11

young carers 8–9
    mental health problems 4
young onset dementia 10–11
young people
    caring for parents with mental health problems 8–9
    and mental health problems 2–4, 29–30
    and mental health services 36
    sleep deprivation 7

ACKNOWLEDGEMENTS

The publisher is grateful for permission to reproduce the following material.

While every care has been taken to trace and acknowledge copyright, the publisher tenders its apology for any accidental infringement or where copyright has proved untraceable. The publisher would be pleased to come to a suitable arrangement in any such case with the rightful owner.

Chapter One: Mental Health Issues

Cost of mental ill health in England exceeds £100 billion, new figures show, © Centre for Mental Health, *Factors that contribute to mental health problems in children and young people,* © Mind, *Mental health: key points,* © The King's Fund, *Six out of ten Britons 'find it difficult to cope mentally',* © Together, *Study reveals sleep duration link to mental ill health,* © George Institute for Global Health, *Young people with parents affected by mental ill health,* © The Princess Royal Trust for Carers, *Younger people with dementia,* © Alzheimer's Society, *Depression linked to dementia,* © Crown copyright is reproduced with the permission of Her Majesty's Stationery Office – nhs.uk, *Bipolar disorder,* © National Institute for Mental Health, *Schizophrenia,* © mentalhealthcare.org.uk, *Dual diagnosis,* © TheSite.org, *Psychosis,* © TheSite.org, *Post Traumatic Stress Disorder (PTSD),* © Combat Stress.

Chapter Two: Mental Illness Stigma

Stigma and discrimination in mental health, © The National Mental Health Development Unit, *The reality of life with a mental health problem,* © Media Wales Ltd., *Myths and facts about mental ill health,* © Sussex Partnership NHS Foundation Time to Change Campaign, *Fear of stigma stops employees with mental health problems from speaking out,* © Rethink, *New intervention to reduce self-stigma among persons with serious mental illness,* © University of Haifa, *With rights in mind,* © Youth Access, *A manifesto for ending mental health stigma,* © Guardian News and Media Limited 2010.

Chapter Three: Surviving Mental Ill Health

How to improve your mental wellbeing, © Mind, *Mental health: strengthening our response,* © World Health Organization, *Young people could fall through mental health care 'gap',* © University of Warwick, *Only one in six people with mental illness receives recommended treatment,* © Rethink, *The Mental Health Act,* © Crown copyright is reproduced with the permission of Her Majesty's Stationery Office.

Illustrations

Pages 1, 9, 26, 36: Simon Kneebone; pages 2, 18, 20, 34: Angelo Madrid; pages 7, 22, 30, 39: Don Hatcher; pages 24, 28: Bev Aisbett.

Cover photography

Left: © Anton Malan. Centre: © Julia Starr. Right: © Christer Rønning Austad (www.christeraustad.com).

Additional acknowledgements

Research and additional editorial by Carolyn Kirby on behalf of Independence.

And with thanks to the Independence team: Mary Chapman, Sandra Dennis and Jan Sunderland.

Lisa Firth
Cambridge
January, 2011

ASSIGNMENTS

The following tasks aim to help you think through the issues surrounding mental health and wellbeing and provide a better understanding of the topic.

1 Brainstorm what you know about mental ill health. Create a mind map to display your ideas, with 'mental wellbeing' at the centre. You might consider these questions: what is mental wellbeing? Who is most at risk of mental health problems? How do mental health disorders impact on everyday living?

2 Read *Factors that contribute to mental health problems in children and young people* on page 2. Choose one of the groups considered susceptible to mental ill health and create an advice leaflet specifically targeting that group. You should provide advice and information on the support that is available for those with mental health problems, including where someone can go for further help.

3 Write a diary entry from the point of view of someone who suffers from a mental illness such as depression. Imagine how they would feel and what challenges they could face in their day-to-day life. You may need to do further research into the mental illness you have chosen.

4 Watch the 2002 film 'The Hours' starring Nicole Kidman. Write a review of the film, discussing how it deals with the subject of depression and mental illness. Do you think it addresses the issue of stigma surrounding mental illness? Did it affect your attitude towards people who suffer from depression or mental ill health?

5 Visit Mind's website at www.mind.org.uk. What are the aims of this organisation? What support do they offer for people suffering from mental health problems? Write a short review of the site, including how accessible you feel the information is and how easy you find the site to use.

6 Read *Bipolar disorder* on pages 14–15. Design a poster to raise awareness of this illness, with the aim of tackling the stigma and discrimination which bipolar sufferers may experience. Your poster will be displayed in schools, hospitals and youth centres so you need to make sure it is eye-catching and informative. You could include details of where people could go for further information, such as the Mind or Mental Health Foundation websites.

7 Read the article *Depression linked to dementia* on pages 12–13. In pairs, create a five- to ten-minute presentation outlining the research: the purpose of the study, the methodology and the findings/conclusions. You can use PowerPoint to prepare your presentation if you wish.

8 Imagine you are an employer looking to fill a vacancy within your company. Someone applies who is well qualified for the job but suffers from bipolar disorder – are there any reasons you might not want someone with this mental illness working for you? In groups of four discuss any reasons you might hesitate to give them the job. Debate this situation for the following job vacancies: a shop assistant; a forklift truck driver; an office manager; a dentist; a teacher. What can your discussion tell you about the stigma people with mental illnesses face in day-to-day life?

9 Visit some online newspaper archives and carry out a search for articles which refer to mental illness. Choose three relevant articles from three different newspapers and analyse the language and terminology they use in discussing mental health. Do the papers vary in their attitude and tone? Based on your research, do you think the media perpetuates the stigma attached to mental illness or discourages it?

10 In groups of seven, stage a quiz show relating to mental wellbeing. Each group should divide into two teams of three people, with one person acting as host. The host should use the myths in the article *Myths and facts about mental ill health* on page 26 as the questions, and teams should state whether they think the myths are true or false. You should discuss any answers you find surprising.

11 Use the statistics given in the key findings on page 27 in the article *Fear of stigma stops employees with mental health problems from speaking out* to create a bar chart. Make sure you label your axes correctly and give the graph a title.

12 'This house believes that people with severe mental illnesses should be cared for in specialist institutions, and not be permitted to live in residential communities as they pose a threat to themselves and others living around them.' Debate this statement in two groups, with one group supporting the statement and the other group opposing.